Athens

DIRECTIONS

WRITTEN AND RESEARCHED BY

John Fisher

ROUGH GUIDES

NEW YORK • LONDON • DELHI
www.roughguides.com

Contents

Introduction to

Athens

For all too many people, Athens is a city that happened two-and-a-half thousand years ago. It's true that even now the past looms large – literally, in the shape of the mighty Acropolis that dominates almost every view, as well as in every visitor's itinerary. Yet the modern city is also home to over four million people – more than a third of the Greek nation's population – and has undergone a transformation in the twenty-first century, partly thanks to the 2004 Olympics, that has made it far more than a repository of antiquities and lifted it above the clichés of pollution and impossible traffic that have blighted its reputation in recent years.

▼ Seafood market

▲ Orthodox priest

There's no denying that the stunning remains of the ancient Classical Greek city are the highlight of any visit. The National Archeological Museum has the finest collection of Greek antiquities in the world, and there are plenty of smaller specialist museums. Even on a brief visit, however, it doesn't do Athens justice to see it purely as a collection of ancient sites and museum pieces.

It's worth taking the time to explore some of the city's neighbourhoods: in particular, the nineteenth-century quarter of Pláka has a delightful mix of Turkish, Neoclassical and Greek island-style architecture along with intriguing little museums. Here you'll also encounter scattered relics of the Byzantine and

When to visit

Athens is at its most agreeable outside the peak period of **early July** to the end of **August**, when soaring temperatures (sometimes over 40°C), plus crowds of visitors, can be overpowering. Perhaps the best months to visit are **May to early June**, **September** and **October** – temperatures are pleasant (20°C and upwards), and visitors fewer. In **April** you can also see lovely displays of spring flowers on the surrounding mountains. The **winter** months can be very cold, and February is often rainy.

medieval town that captivated Byron and the Romantics. Just to the north, the bazaar area retains an almost Middle Eastern atmosphere, with the added bonus of some of the city's best nightlife in neighbouring Psyrrí and up-and-coming Gázi. More traditional Athenian escapes are also nearby in the form of the shady National Gardens and the elegant, upmarket quarter of Kolonáki. There are also startling views to be enjoyed from the many hills – Lykavitós and Filopáppou in particular – while in summer, the beach is just a tram-ride away.

Further out, in easy reach of day-trips, are more Classical sites – Soúnio and Delphi above all – opportunities to walk in the mountains that surround the city, and the chance to escape to the islands, several of which can be reached from the busy port of Pireás in just a couple of hours.

The biggest surprise in Athens for most people, however, is the vibrant life of the city itself. Cafés are packed day and night, and the streets stay lively until 3 or 4am, with some of the best bars and clubs in the country. Eating out is great, with establishments ranging from lively tavernas to the finest gourmet restaurants. In summer much of the action takes place outdoors, complemented by open-air films, concerts and classical drama. There's a diverse shopping scene, too, ranging from colourful bazaars and lively

▼ Hadrian's Library

▲ Bar in Gázi

street markets to chic shopping malls filled with the latest designer goods. And with a good-value, extensive public transport system allied to inexpensive cabs, you'll have no difficulty getting around.

▼ The sprawl

Athens
AT A GLANCE

THE NATIONAL ARCHEO-LOGICAL MUSEUM

By far the most important museum in Athens, the National Archeological Museum houses the world's greatest collection of Cycladic, Minoan, Mycenaean and Classical Greek art.

▲ Sculptures at the National Archeological Museum

THE ACROPOLIS

The Acropolis remains the city's biggest attraction. Dominating its southern slope is the restored second-century Roman Herodes Atticus Theatre, a spectacular setting for performances of music and Classical drama during the summer festival.

PSYRRÍ

The focus of the city's nightlife, Psyrrí is home to a throng of ever-changing cafés, bars and *mezedhopolío*.

DELPHI

Set amongst the massive crags of Mount Parnassós, Delphi is the site of the most important oracle in ancient Greece. Today, its awe-inspiring ruins and spectacular setting make it one of the most memorable excursions from Athens.

▼ Bar in Psyrrí

▲ Cape Soúnio

CAPE SOÚNIO

Cape Soúnio's dramatic setting overlooking the Aegean has, for centuries, made it a landmark to boats sailing between Pireás and the islands. Its tremendous views and evocative Temple of Poseidon certainly impressed Byron, who carved his name on one of the pillars.

PLÁKA

The largely pedestrianized area of Pláka, with its narrow lanes and stepped alleys climbing towards the Acropolis, are perhaps the most attractive part of Athens. This is the place to simply wander around: touristy but full of atmosphere.

MONASTIRÁKI

While less touristy and more commercial than Pláka, Monastiráki still has great opportunities for eating, drinking and, above all, shopping – from flea markets to alternative fashion.

▼ Shopping in Monastiráki

Ideas

The big six

Athens is still defined above all by the brief period of glory it enjoyed in the fifth century BC – the Golden Age of Classical Athens. The signature image of the city, and an absolute must-see, is the rocky hill of the Acropolis, topped by the Parthenon. Smaller, lesser-known ancient sites are scattered throughout the city centre. The city's Archeological Museum, too, is one of the world's greatest, with treasures not just from Athens but from all the cultures of ancient Greece. The modern city, meanwhile, may not always be beautiful, but it is raucously alive, with its buzzing outdoor restaurants and cafés, great nightlife, and easy access to a spectacular coastline.

▲ Street life

In summer, life in Athens moves on to the streets, terraces and roof gardens. Dining or drinking al fresco, often with the Acropolis as backdrop, can be an unforgettable experience.

P.82 ▸ MONASTIRÁKI AND PSYRRÍ

▼ National Archeological Museum

The world's finest collection of Classical Greek sculpture adorns Athens' premier museum.

P.111 ▸ THE ARCHEOLOGICAL MUSEUM, EXÁRHIA AND NEÁPOLI

▼ Lykavitós Hill

Climb Lykavitós Hill – or take the funicular – for spectacular views of the city, including the Acropolis.

P.121 ▸ KOLONÁKI AND LYKAVITÓS HILL

▼ Tower of the Winds

On the site of the Roman Forum, the intriguing and well-preserved Tower of the Winds is compass, weather vane, sundial and water-clock in one.

P.69 ▸ PLÁKA

▲ Temple of Poseidon

Dominating Cape Soúnio, the Temple of Poseidon commands magnificent views of the seas and islands around Athens.

P.144 ▸ AROUND ATHENS

▲ Acropolis

Crowned by the Parthenon, and surrounded by the major relics of ancient Athens, the Acropolis is one of the archetypal images of Western civilization.

P.51 ▸ THE ACROPOLIS

Acropolis

Exploring the Acropolis and its surrounds can easily absorb an entire day. While the Parthenon is the most imposing of the remains atop the steep-sided hill, it's far from the only one; the Acropolis has an extraordinary concentration of superlative Classical architecture, all of it dating from just a few decades at the height of ancient Athenian democracy. The Acropolis Museum houses many of the treasures from the site and hopes one day to complete its collection with the returned Parthenon Marbles.

▲ The Erechtheion

The most sacred of the ancient temples and a superb example of Ionic architecture, the Erechtheion's south porch is supported by six larger-than-life maidens – the Caryatids.

P.57 ▶ THE ACROPOLIS

▲ Acropolis Museum

Containing almost all the treasures removed from the site since the 1830s, the museum includes fine sculptures that once adorned the Acropolis buildings.

P.58 ▶ THE ACROPOLIS

▶ Acropolis by night

The Acropolis is spectacularly lit at night throughout the summer, effects that can be enjoyed from vantage points across the city.

P.51 ▶ THE ACROPOLIS

▲ The Parthenon Marbles

Part of the pediment of the Parthenon has been reconstructed in the Acropolis Museum – although the Elgin Marbles remain in the British Museum, despite a long Greek campaign to reclaim them.

P.57 ▶ THE ACROPOLIS

▼ The Propylaia

The imposing entrance to the Acropolis now as in Classical times, the Propylaia were considered by ancient Athenians to be their most prestigious monument.

P.53 ▶ THE ACROPOLIS

Golden Age Athens

In the fifth century BC, the city-state of Athens suddenly found itself secure and wealthy, having defeated the Persians and risen to dominate its mainland rivals. The Athenians celebrated their success by a radical experiment with democracy, and with a flourishing of art, architecture, literature and philosophy whose influences imbue Western culture to this day. The physical remains of the Classical Golden Age are still to be seen everywhere in Athens, and with the city's reconstruction more is emerging almost daily.

▲ Stoa of Attalos

The reconstruction of the Stoa of Attalos, part of the ancient Athenian marketplace, shows how Classical Athens might have looked in its heyday, and houses the Museum of the Agora.

P.62 ▸ THE ACROPOLIS

▼ Theatre of Dionysos

As evocative a setting as any in Athens, the theatre witnessed the first productions of the masterpieces of Classical drama by Aeschylus, Sophocles, Euripides and Aristophanes.

P.59 ▸ THE ACROPOLIS

▲ Kerameikos

A tranquil, little-visited site that incorporates the cemetery of ancient Athens as well as fragments of the city walls, gates and the roads that led to them.

P.90 ▸ THISSÍO, GÁZI AND ÁNO PETRÁLONA

▼ Hephaisteion

The Temple of Hephaistos – God of Fire – is among the best preserved of all the ancient temples in Athens.

P.61 ▸ THE ACROPOLIS

Roman Athens

The Romans controlled Athens for some eight hundred years, but they left relatively few monuments. On the whole they respected the artistic and architectural heritage of Classical Athens, while the city itself became something of a backwater of the Empire. There were, however, two great benefactors in particular whose legacy has survived: the Emperor Hadrian and Herodes Atticus, a wealthy Roman senator.

▲ Hadrian's Arch

Erected by Hadrian to mark the division between the ancient Greek city and the modern Roman one, this imposing arch rises to a height of eighteen metres.

P.99 ▸ SÝNDAGMA AND AROUND

▼ The Areopagus

In Roman times St Paul preached on this low, rocky hill, setting in train the conversion of Athens to Christianity. It's rich in other history too, and in ancient times was the site of the Council of Nobles and the Judicial Court.

P.60 ▸ THE ACROPOLIS

▶ Hadrian's Library

The emperor's monument – not merely a library but an entire cultural centre – was built on a truly impressive scale, and even in ruins the size is awesome.

P.77 ▶ MONASTIRÁKI AND PSYRRÍ

◀ The Roman Forum

Built by Julius and Augustus Caesar as an extension of the busy Greek marketplace, the Roman Forum is one of the main attractions in Monastiráki. The site includes the oldest Mosque in Athens, the Fethiye Tzami.

P.68 ▶ MONASTIRÁKI AND PSYRRÍ

▼ Odeion of Herodes Atticus

The partly reconstructed theatre at the foot of the Acropolis is today a stunning setting for events at the annual Hellenic festival.

P.59 ▶ THE ACROPOLIS

Byzantine Athens

When the Roman empire split, Athens came under the control of Byzantium (Constantinople) and the Byzantine empire. The schools of philosophy were closed, and many of the city's "pagan" temples converted to churches. The legacy of the early Christians is a series of beautiful ancient monasteries, as well as museums and wonderful frescoes and icons.

▼ Mosaic floors

Many early churches had decorative mosaic flooring: this example is preserved in the Byzantine Museum, while others have recently been excavated in the Hadrian's Library site.

P.124 ▶ KOLONÁKI AND LYKAVITÓS HILL

▼ Icons

Religious icons are perhaps the greatest art produced by the Orthodox Church; there are many wonderful examples in the Byzantine Museum, and reproductions on sale at religious paraphernalia shops throughout the city.

P.125 ▶ KOLONÁKI AND LYKAVITÓS HILL

▲ Kessarianí Monastery

A haven of peace in the suburbs, the monastery at Kessarianí has beautiful frescoes, and grounds from which you can set off to walk in the mountains above the city.

P.142 ▶ AROUND ATHENS

▼ Byzantine and Christian Museum

This refurbished museum has a magnificent display of Byzantine artworks: mosaics, frecoes, icons and much more.

P.124 ▶ KOLONÁKI AND LYKAVITÓS HILL

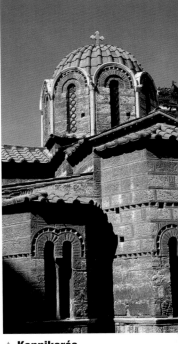

▲ Kapnikaréa

The eleventh-century church of Kapnikaréa, right in the heart of Athens, makes for an extraordinary contrast to the packed shopping streets surrounding it.

P.79 ▶ MONASTIRÁKI AND PSYRRÍ

Archeological Museum

Athens' National Archeological Museum is among the world's greatest museums, with an unrivalled collection of ancient Greek art. It spans every era from prehistoric and the development of Mycenaean and Minoan culture, through Classical Greece and on to Roman and early Byzantine times. Extensive renovation for the 2004 Olympics has provided a setting to match the contents. Highlights include the finds from graves at Mycenae, and from the island of Thíra (Santorini), as well as a truly fabulous sculpture collection.

▲ Poseidon

In this graceful bronze statue from the mid-fifth century BC, Poseidon stands poised in perfect balance as he prepares to hurl his (missing) trident.

P.111 ▶ THE ARCHEOLOGICAL MUSEUM, EXÁRHIA AND NEÁPOLI

▲ Frescoes

Upstairs are galleries devoted to the excavations at Akrotíri on Thíra, and above all some of the famous frescoes found there, their style clearly influenced by Minoan Crete.

P.111 ▶ THE ARCHEOLOGICAL MUSEUM, EXÁRHIA AND NEÁPOLI

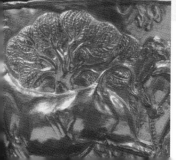

▶ The Vafio Cup

This wonderful gold cup, one of two dating from around 1500 BC, depicts a bull being trapped, and was made by beating the gold into a hollow mould.

P.111 ▶ THE ARCHEOLOGICAL MUSEUM, EXÁRHIA AND NEÁPOLI

◀ The Little Jockey of Artemission

In another masterpiece of animated bronze sculpture, the delicate-looking rider – probably a boy – seems far too small for his galloping mount.

P.111 ▶ THE ARCHEOLOGICAL MUSEUM, EXÁRHIA AND NEÁPOLI

▼ The museum building

The imposing Neoclassical building housing the Museum, newly refurbished, occupies an entire block, set back from the street .

P.111 ▶ THE ARCHEOLOGICAL MUSEUM, EXÁRHIA AND NEÁPOLI

Athens museums

The city's lesser-known museums should not be overlooked. Among the best are the Benáki and Kanellopoulou museums, each housing magnificent private collections that cover every age of Greek art and history from the prehistoric era to the nineteenth-century independence struggle. Others are more specialist: for example, the Goulandhrís Museum of Cycladic Art concentrates on artefacts predating the Classical era, superbly displayed, while the Museum of Greek Folk Art features ceramics, jewellery, weaving and other crafts.

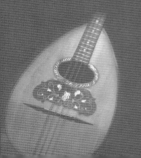

▲ Goulandhrís Museum of Cycladic and Ancient Greek Art

Another private collection, notable above all for its extensive collection of Cycladic art, whose style influenced many early twentieth-century artists.

P.123 ▸ KOLONÁKI AND LYKAVITÓS HILL

▲ Museum of Greek Popular Musical Instruments

Superbly displayed in a Neoclassical building, the museum traces the history of virtually every type of instrument ever played in Greece.

P.90 ▸ PLÁKA

▲ Kanellopoulou Museum

Right under the Acropolis at the top of Pláka, the Kanellopoulou Museum fills a former private home with a treasure-trove of fine art.

P.67 ▸ PLÁKA

▼ Museum of Greek Folk Art

A comprehensive collection of arts and crafts, including regional costumes and shadow puppets.

P.68 ▸ PLÁKA

▲ Benáki Museum

Housed in a graceful nineteenth-century mansion, the Benáki collection is of exceptional variety and quality.

P.123 ▸ KOLONÁKI AND LYKAVITÓS HILL

Ottoman Athens

Greece was under Turkish control as part of the Ottoman Empire for almost 400 years, right up until the mid-nineteenth century. Until recently, though, this era was hidden away, and most traces of the "occupation" deliberately erased in a bid to assert Greek nationhood. Today, in an atmosphere of improving relations between modern Turkey and modern Greece, some light is at last being thrown on this lost era.

▲ The bazaar

Perhaps the most lasting legacy of the Turks can be felt in the streets around the central market, where small shops are still organized on the basis of an Oriental *souk*, each area specializing in particular goods.

P.102 ▸ PLATÍA OMONÍAS AND THE BAZAAR

▼ Fethiye Tzami

The oldest mosque in Athens is now used as a store-room in the Roman Forum archeological site. At least that humble usage has ensured the building's survival.

P.69 ▸ PLÁKA

▲ Turkish baths

These baths – there were once many others – were in use right up to the 1960s, and have now been lovingly restored and opened as a museum.

P.69 ▸ PLÁKA

▼ Ceramics Collection

This branch of the Museum of Greek Folk Art is housed in a historic mosque. The building is at least as interesting as its contents.

P.77 ▸ MONASTIRÁKI AND PSYRRÍ

▲ Benáki Museum of Islamic Art

Jammed with beautiful, intricately decorated objects, the new Islamic Art Museum does exactly what it says on the label.

P.90 ▸ THISSÍO, GÁZI AND ÁNO PETRÁLONA

Hills and views

Athens is dotted with hills and surrounded by mountains, almost all of which offer great views and the opportunity to escape the clamour of the city for a while. Inevitably, the Acropolis seems to find its way into every photo, but there are fine cityscapes to be enjoyed in other directions too. The Acropolis itself offers good views of the city, while Lykavitós is the other classic viewpoint – with the added advantage of a walk through elegant Kolonáki and a funicular to get you to the toP. On the fringes of the city, the mountains of Imittós and Párnitha are surprisingly rugged – making them excellent hiking territory.

▲ Lófos tou Stréfi

Stréfi Hill is little visited and offers a quiet escape from the streets of surrounding Exárhia.

P.113 ▸ THE ARCHEOLOGICAL MUSEUM, EXÁRHIA AND NEÁPOLI

▲ Filopáppou

Filopáppou Hill, romantically known in antiquity as the Hill of the Muses, is topped by a grandiose monument to the Roman senator after whom it is named. It's seen here from the Acropolis, with the Herodes Atticus Theatre in the foreground.

P.87 ▸ THISSÍO, GÁZI AND ÁNO PETRÁLONA

▲ Lykavitós

From the top, Athens is laid out before you in all directions – on a clear day you can see as far as the mountains of the Peloponnese.

P.121 ▸ KOLONÁKI AND LYKAVITÓS HILL

▶ The Pnyx

The remains of the ancient Athenian assembly stand at the summit of the Hill of the Pnyx.

P.87 ▸ THISSÍO, GÁZI AND ÁNO PETRÁLONA

▼ The Acropolis

No matter where you are, the Acropolis seems to dominate the view: it is especially dramatic looking across the city towards Pireás, and the constant movement of shipping in the waters beyond.

P.51 ▸ THE ACROPOLIS

Green Athens

At first sight Athens is not a green city, but it has its moments. The citizens decorate their balconies with potted plants and shrubs, while in the older quarters bougainvillea covers many houses. In spring, flowers try to blossom everywhere – archeological sites and the steeper slopes of the hills are ideal breeding grounds. At the very heart of the city, the National Gardens offer almost tropical luxuriance, while as soon as you leave the city limits, nature reasserts itself immediately, whether in the mountains, the coast or the nearby islands.

▲ The National Gardens

Part formally laid out, part distinctly over-grown, the National Gardens make for a refreshing, shady escape from the summer heat.

`P.98` ▸ SÝNDAGMA AND AROUND

▼ Égina

The rural island of Égina, less than an hour by hydrofoil from Athens, is famed above all for its pistachios, lush orchards of which spread across the interior.

`P.163` ▸ FURTHER AFIELD

▲ Lykavitós

The lower slopes of Lykavitós and many of the city's other hills are covered in pine trees and succulents; despite appearances, it's a fairly easy walk uP.

P.121 ▸ KOLONÁKI AND LYKAVITÓS HILL

▼ Ruins in spring

Even in the heart of Athens, in springtime flowers burst through and adorn the many ancient remains.

P.51 ▸ THE ACROPOLIS

Restaurants and tavernas

Athens has a huge variety of restaurants and tavernas. The atmosphere is invariably relaxed, though the city does have its share of fancy places. There's virtually every type of cuisine too, but the vast majority of places, and the ones most frequented by locals, remain no-frills tavernas. Most menus are simple, but you can rely on good-quality, fresh ingredients: if you're not sure about the menu, you can often go into the kitchen and see what's on offer. A typically Greek way to eat is to order a selection of small dishes – *mezédhes* – to share.

▲ Taverna music

Evening performances of traditional Greek music are common, and while often rather touristy they are occasionally great. These guys are playing at the *Taverna tou Psarra*.

P.72 ▶ PLÁKA

▼ Pláka

Most Athens restaurants have a terrace, courtyard or stretch of pavement on which tables are set up outside in summer. The steep pedestrian streets of Pláka provide a particularly atmospheric setting.

P.71 ▶ PLÁKA

Εστιατόριο Eden®

▶ Áno Petrálona

Away from the touristy central districts, neighbourhoods such as Áno Petrálona generally offer more authentic menus and a more local atmosphere.

P.92 ▸ THISSÍO, GÁZI AND ÁNO PETRÁLONA

◀ Baïraktaris

Straightforward, inexpensive traditional Greek food ensures that *Baïraktaris* is always packed.

P.83 ▸ MONASTIRÁKI AND PSYRRÍ

▼ Eden

Catering for Athens' vegetarians for decades now, *Eden* is enduringly popular.

P.72 ▸ PLÁKA

▼ Dhiporto

Athens dining as it used to be: a barely marked pavement dive, packed for long lunches with people from all walks of life.

P.108 ▸ PLATÍA OMONÍAS AND THE BAZAAR

Cafés and bars

There seems to be a café on every corner in Athens, most of which open from mid-morning till late in the evening. They're an essential part of the social fabric of the city, always full of groups of people chatting (on their mobiles if not to each other), smoking and drinking. Join them over a Greek coffee or the quintessential summer drink, a frappé: iced instant coffee, whipped to a froth. If you fancy a cold beer, you can have that in a café too – many effectively become fancy and expensive bars in the evening, when they turn down the lights and turn up the music.

▲ Athinalon Politeia

The terrace views of the Acropolis from the *Athinalon Politeia* café are the equal of any in the city. The perfect place to start your evening.

P.92 ▶ THISSÍO, GÁZI AND ÁNO PETRÁLONA

▼ Kolonáki

The cafés of upmarket Kolonáki are the ultimate expression of Athenian café life: always crowded with an ever-changing cast.

P.128 ▶ KOLONÁKI AND LYKAVITÓS HILL

▼ Brettos

Backlit bottles decorate *Brettos*, a perennial Pláka favourite that's a liquor store by day and bar at night.

P.75 ▸ PLÁKA

▲ Psyrrí

By night, Psyrrí can boast some of the city's trendiest bars and restaurants, while by day it's a relaxing place for a coffee.

P.85 ▸ MONASTIRÁKI AND PSYRRÍ

▼ Thissío

Thissío has a real buzz to it at night – a revitalized area whose bars and cafés draw a predominantly young crowd.

P.95 ▸ THISSÍO, GÁZI AND ÁNO PETRÁLONA

Music and entertainment

To see the best live traditional Greek music, perhaps surprisingly you need to visit during the winter months, as in the summer many musicians are off touring the country. This is also when the major ballet and drama performances are staged, and the sporting calendar is at its busiest. The summer, however, is the festival season, and most important of all is the June-to-September Hellenic Festival of dance, music and ancient drama, with many of its performances staged in the ancient theatres of Herodes Atticus and Epidaurus. Annual rock, jazz and blues events are also a summer staple.

▲ Rebétika

Rebétika, the drugs-and-outcast music brought to Athens by Greeks from Asia Minor in the early twentieth century, is still close to the heart of most Athenians, and the basis of the traditional music you'll hear at clubs and tavernas across the city.

P.75 ▸ MONASTIRÁKI AND PSYRRÍ

▼ Gagarin 205

The city's finest indoor live-rock venue hosts touring indie bands as well as home-grown talent.

P.118 ▸ THE ARCHEOLOGICAL MUSEUM, EXÁRHIA AND NEÁPOLI

▶ Hellenic Festival

The annual Hellenic Festival features cultural events across the city, but above all performances, including ancient Greek drama, at the restored theatres of Herodes Atticus and at Epidauros.

P.159 ▸ PLATÍA OMONÍAS AND THE BAZAAR

▲ Stoa Athanaton

One of the longest-established traditional music clubs in the city, the *Stoa Athanaton* is busy right through winter, with a regular company of accomplished musicians.

P.109 ▸ PLATÍA OMONÍAS AND THE BAZAAR

▼ Lykavitós Theatre

The open-air theatre perched atop Lykavitós is a spectacular venue. Many of the city's major rock events are staged here.

P.123 ▸ KOLONÁKI AND LYKAVITÓS HILL

Nightlife

Clubs and dance bars are hugely popular in Athens, and often extremely sophisticated. Downtown, the hottest action is in the Psyrrí and Gázi areas, but in summer many close down and decamp to a string of hangar-like places on the coastal strip from Pireás to Várkiza. Expect the unexpected: most play recent hits, but don't be surprised if the sound shifts to Greek or belly-dancing music towards the end of the night. The gay scene in Athens is mostly very discreet, but there is an increasing number of clubs and bars; Gázi is the hottest new area, while more established places are mostly in Kolonáki or off Syngroú Avenue.

▲ Beach clubs

Beachside clubs and bars open up in summer to cater to the clubbers seeking the cooler climes of the coast. *Envy Mediterraneo*, seen here, is one of the biggest.

P.154 ▸ AROUND ATHENS

▼ Cubanita

Cuban theme and a party atmosphere in the heart of downtown Psyrrí.

P.85 ▸ MONASTIRÁKI AND PSYRRÍ

▲ Balthazar

The glamorous setting in an old mansion and its garden attracts a more mature, well-heeled crowd of late-night clubbers.

P.129 ▸ KOLONÁKI AND LYKAVITÓS HILL

▼ Gázi

Up-and-coming Gázi has some of the best clubs downtown – its old industrial buildings offering great warehouse-style space. The rooftop bar at *45° Mires* is a great place to start your night.

P.95 ▸ THISSÍO, GÁZI AND ÁNO PETRÁLONA

▲ Mooi Bar

Typically cool designer bar in Psyrrí, a great place to meet up at the beginning of the evening, or to chill out in later.

P.85 ▸ MONASTIRÁKI AND PSYRRÍ

Markets and shopping

Shopping in Athens is decidedly schizophrenic. On the one hand, the bazaar area is an extraordinary jumble of little specialist shops and stalls, while almost every neighbourhood still hosts a weekly street market. On the other, the upmarket shopping areas of the city centre, and the malls and fashion emporia of the ritzier suburbs, are as glossy and expensive as any in Europe. The food halls of the central market and the picturesque flower market nearby are particularly worthwhile, while if you're into trawling through junk, don't miss the Sunday-morning flea markets in Monastiráki and Pireás.

▲ The fish market

Seafood and fish play a big part in the Athenian diet, and at the bustling fish market you'll see residents and taverna owners alike browsing the catch.

P.104 ▸ PLATÍAS OMONÍAS AND THE BAZAAR

▼ Kiosks

Handy for anything from newspapers to cold drinks, tobacco and any manner of essentials, kiosks are found on every corner and stay open all hours. Several in Omónia specialize in the foreign press.

P.105 ▸ PLATÍA OMONÍAS AND THE BAZAAR

▼ Street markets

Street markets held across the city are great places to stock up on picnic fare and get a taste of local Athens.

P.130 ▸ MAKRIYIÁNNI, KOUKÁKI, PANGRÁTI AND METS

▼ Kolonáki

For shopaholics with money to spend, Kolonáki's chic shopping streets and fashion boutiques are the place to head.

P.119 ▸ KOLONÁKI AND LYKAVITÓS HILL

▲ Monastiráki flea market

The "flea market" is actually a crowded area of shops and stalls, but it's fun to browse and on Sunday mornings you'll still find a real flea market in the surrounding streets.

P.78 ▸ MONASTIRÁKI AND PSYRRÍ

Orthodox Athens

Over ninety-five percent of the Greek population describe themselves as Orthodox, and the rituals of the Orthodox Church constantly permeate everyday life – often going completely unnoticed. For all its surface modernity, Athens is no exception. Taxi drivers cross themselves as they pass a church, mid-flow in an animated discussion of last night's match; shoppers pop into the church and light a candle before continuing with their errands; and lamps are lit daily in front of icons in most homes. Religious festivals are celebrated with gusto, and weddings, baptisms and funerals draw huge crowds of extended family.

▲ Historic icons

When you've had your fill of browsing the icon shops, check out their historic predecessors at the Byzantine and Christian Museum.

P.125 ▸ KOLONÁKI AND LYKAVITÓS HILL

▲ Platía Mitropóleos

The quiet square itself is more of a draw than the cathedral here, but there has been a church on this site for centuries.

P.80 ▸ MONASTIRÁKI AND PSYRRÍ

▲ Easter

Easter is by far the most important festival of the Orthodox year – much bigger than Christmas – and is fervently celebrated throughout the city. The midnight service on Easter Saturday is the highlight.

P.184 ▸ ESSENTIALS

▼ Icon shops

Icons, from cheap reproductions aimed at the tourist market to expensive and exquisite copies are sold everywhere. Some of the best are found in the religious-artefact shops around Platía Mitropóleos.

P.81 ▸ MONASTIRÁKI AND PSYRRÍ

Athens on foot

Central Athens is compact enough to be able to walk almost anywhere. One of the lasting legacies of the 2004 Olympics is the network of pedestrian streets that transformed the centre of town. Quite apart from the pleasure of being able to witness the ancient sites from a traffic-free environment, pedestrianization, together with the extension of the metro and other public-transport initiatives, have helped dramatically reduce Athens' critical pollution problems.

▲ Odhós Ermoú

A traffic-free route from Sýndagma to Monastiráki, Ermoú is also one of the prime shopping streets in the centre.

P.76 ▸ MONASTIRÁKI AND PSYRRÍ

▼ Apóstolou Pávlou

Part of the pedestrian route that circles the Agora and Acropolis, Apostólou Pávlou has great views, as well as access to the cafés and bars of Thissío or the quieter pleasures of the hills of the Pnyx and Filopáppou.

P.86 ▸ THISSÍO, GÁZI AND ÁNO PETRÁLONA

▼ Kolonáki

From the shopping streets in the heart of Kolonáki you can climb steeply towards Lykavitós Hill – or do it the easy way and take the funicular up and walk down.

P.119 ▶ KOLONÁKI AND LYKAVITÓS HILL

▲ Odhós Adhrianoú

From Thissío metro all the way through Pláka, Adhrianoú is lined with bustling cafés and shops.

P.79 ▶ MONASTIRÁKI AND PSYRRÍ

▼ Dhionysíou Areopayítou

A relaxed, traffic-free street on the south side of the Acropolis, passing the Herodes Atticus Theatre.

P.86 ▶ THE ACROPOLIS

Seaside Athens and island escapes

Athens is surrounded by the sea, and the Greek nation has a seafaring tradition going back to Classical times. There are some great beaches in easy reach, though on summer weekends they're packed to capacity. At many of the best you pay for entry, allowing you to use a range of facilities from loungers to water sports. More adventurously, from the port of Pireás you can get a ferry to one of a number of nearby islands, escaping in just a couple of hours (half that if you take a hydrofoil) to an entirely different world.

▲ Náfplio

The beautiful old town of Náfplio, with its picturesque castles, attracts plenty of week-ending Athenians, ensuring lively nightlife to go with the sights.

P.160 ▸ FURTHER AFIELD

▲ Temple of Afaia, Égina

The rural island of Égina seems another world – the serene Temple of Afaia can be reached by a good local bus service.

P.163 ▸ FURTHER AFIELD

▲ Ferries from Pireás

Part of the magic of visiting the islands is the journey itself; an impressive array of ferries, catamarans and hydrofoils offer a smooth crossing as they run between the bustling port and the islands.

P.139 ▸ AROUND ATHENS

▼ Póros

Póros lies in close proximity to the mainland, ensuring a steady stream of customers for its fine waterfront restaurants and cafés.

P.163 ▸ FURTHER AFIELD

▼ Beach at Glyfádha

Athens' suburban beaches may be busy, but they offer plenty of facilities, and above all clean sand and sparkling sea.

P.141 ▸ AROUND ATHENS

Out of Athens

Attica, the province surrounding Athens, has numerous attractions beyond the obvious ones offered by its beaches: above all, important outposts of Classical Athens, made all the more appealing now by their rural isolation. Further out, some of the great sites, including Delphi and Mycenae, are an easy day-triP. The mountains, with their traditional villages, walking and even skiing opportunities, are yet another alternative.

▼ Delphi

Delphi, home of the Delphic Oracle, was thought by the ancient Greeks to be the centre of the earth. It's still among the most impressive of all ancient sites.

P.155 ▸ FURTHER AFIELD

▲ Temple of Poseidon

Cape Soúnio and the beautiful temple that stands at its tip have long been a landmark for sailors approaching Athens.

P.144 ▸ AROUND ATHENS

▼ Mycenae

The discovery of Mycenae in the late nineteenth century was a seminal event in Greek archeology, proving that Homer and the stories of ancient, pre-Classical civilizations were not mere myth.

P.162 ▶ FURTHER AFIELD

▲ Skhiniás

Skhiniás beach, on the east coast near ancient Marathon, is probably the best within easy reach of the capital; for once there's a chance of escaping the crowds.

P.147 ▶ AROUND ATHENS

▼ Eleusis

The Sanctuary of Demeter at Eleusis – accessible by city bus from Athens – was one of the most important in the ancient world.

P.146 ▶ AROUND ATHENS

Places

The Acropolis

The rock of the Acropolis, crowned by the dramatic ruins of the Parthenon, is one of the archetypal images of Western culture. The first time you see it, rising above the traffic or from a distant hill, is extraordinary: foreign and yet utterly familiar. The Parthenon temple was always intended to be a landmark, and was famous throughout the ancient world. Yet even in their wildest dreams its creators could hardly have imagined that the ruins would come to symbolize the emergence of Western civilization – nor that, two-and-a-half millennia on, it would attract some three million tourists a year.

The Acropolis itself is simply the rock on which the monuments are built; almost every ancient Greek city had its acropolis (which means the summit or highest point of the city), but the acropolis of Athens is The Acropolis, the one that needs no further introduction. Its natural setting, a steep-sided, flat-topped crag of limestone rising abruptly a hundred metres from its surroundings, has made it the focus of the city during every phase of its development. Easily defensible and with plentiful water, its initial attractions are obvious – even now, with no function apart from tourism, it is the undeniable heart of the city, around which everything else clusters, glimpsed at almost every turn.

Crowds at the Acropolis can be horrendous – to avoid the worst, come very early or late in the day. The peak rush usually comes in late morning,

▼ PARTHENON

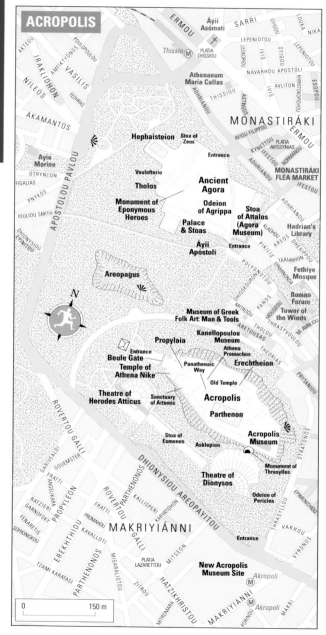

ACROPOLIS

Acropolis tickets and opening times

A joint ticket (€12; free to under-18s and EU students; €6 for non-EU students and EU citizens over 65; free on public holidays and Sundays Nov–March) covers the Acropolis, Ancient Agora and South Slope, plus the Roman Forum, Kerameikos and the Temple of Olympian Zeus. The smaller sites also offer individual tickets, but only the joint one is valid for the summit of the Acropolis, so if you visit any of the others first, be sure to buy the multiple ticket or you simply end up paying twice. It can be used over four days, although there doesn't seem to be any way of indicating when it was issued.

The Acropolis, South Slope (individual entry €2) and Ancient Agora (individual entry €4) are **open** daily April–Sept 8am–7.30pm, Oct–March 8am–4.30pm.

when coach tours congregate before moving on to lunch elsewhere. The sites included in this chapter fall within one of three separate fenced areas: the summit of the Acropolis, which includes the Parthenon itself, the Propylaia – the gateway through which the ancient sanctuary was entered – the Acropolis Museum, and other temples including the Erechtheion and the Temple of Athena Nike; the South Slope with its two great theatres; and the Ancient Agora. There are no shops or restaurants within the Acropolis area, although you can buy water and sandwiches, guidebooks, postcards and so on from a couple of stands near the Beule Gate. There's also a handy branch of Everest right opposite Akrópoli metro station (at the corner of Mariyiánni and Dhiakoú) and plenty of similar places around Monastiráki metro. If you want to sit down, there are cafés and tavernas nearby in almost every direction: see Pláka (p.71), Monastiráki (p.82), Makriyiánni (p.134) and Thissío (p.92).

The Propylaia

Main Acropolis site. Today, as throughout history, the Propylaia are the gateway to the Acropolis. In Classical times the road extended along a steep ramp to this monumental double-gatehouse; the modern path makes a more gradual, zigzagging ascent, passing first through an arched Roman entrance, the Beule Gate, added in the third century AD.

▼ PROPYLAIA

Approaches to the Acropolis

The sites are ringed by a pedestrian walkway, allowing views of the Parthenon to be appreciated from almost every angle. You may get a little lost among the jumble of alleys in Pláka, but the rock itself is always there to guide you. The Acropolis can be entered only from the west, where there's a big coach-park at the bottom of the hill.

On foot, the most common approach to the ruins is from the northwest corner of Pláka, on a path that extends above Odhós Dhioskoúron where it joins Theorías. You can also approach from the south, where pedestrianized Dhionysíou Areopayítou (Metro Akrópoli) offers access to the South Slope; from the north via the Ancient Agora (entrance on Adhrianoú; Metro Monastiráki); or, slightly further but repaid with excellent views of both Agora and Acropolis, from Thissío along traffic-free Apostólou Pávlou (Metro Thissío).

The Propylaia were constructed by Mnesikles from 437–432 BC, and their axis and proportions aligned to balance the recently completed Parthenon. They were built from the same marble as the temple, and in grandeur and architectural achievement are almost as impressive. The ancient Athenians, awed by the fact that such wealth and craftsmanship should be used for a purely secular building, ranked this as their most prestigious monument.

Walking through the gateway, which would originally have had great wooden doors, is your only chance to enter any of the ancient buildings atop the Acropolis. To the left of the central hall (which before Venetian bombardment supported a great coffered roof, painted blue and gilded with stars), the Pinakotheke was an early art gallery, exhibiting paintings of Homeric subjects by Polygnotus. The wing to the right is much smaller, as Mnesikles's original design incorporated ground sacred to the Goddess of Victory and the premises had to be adapted as a waiting room for her shrine – the Temple of Athena Nike.

The Panathenaic Way

Main Acropolis site. The Panathenaic Way was the route of the great annual procession for ancient Athens' Panathenaic Festival, in honour of the city's patron goddess Athena. The procession – depicted on the Parthenon frieze – wound right through the Classical city from the gates now in the Kerameikos site (p.90) via the Propylaia to the Parthenon and, finally, the Erechtheion. One of the best-preserved stretches of the ancient route, which was used as a road between festivals too, can be seen just inside the Propylaia. Here you can make out grooves cut for footholds in the rock and, to either side, niches for innumerable statues and offerings. In Classical times it ran past a ten-metre-high bronze statue of *Athena Promachos* (Athena the Champion), whose base can just about be made out. Athena's spear and helmet were said to be visible to sailors approaching from as far away as Soúnio. The statue was moved to Constantinople in Byzantine times and later destroyed.

The Temple of Athena Nike

Main Acropolis site. Simple and

A brief history of the Acropolis

The rocky Acropolis was home to one of the earliest known settlements in Greece, its slopes inhabited by a **Neolithic** community around 5000 BC. In **Mycenaean** times – around 1500 BC – it was fortified with massive walls, parts of which can still be seen, enclosing a royal palace and temples to the goddess Athena. By the ninth century BC, the Acropolis had become the heart of Athens, the first Greek city-state, sheltering its principal public buildings.

Most of the substantial remains seen today date from the **fifth century BC** or later, by which time the buildings here were purely religious. The earlier buildings were burned to the ground when the Persians sacked Athens in 480 BC. Following peace with Persia in 449 BC the walls were rebuilt and plans drawn up for a reconstruction worthy of the city's cultural and political position. This vast project, coinciding with the Golden Age of Classical Athens, was masterminded by **Pericles** and carried out under the general direction of the architect and sculptor **Fidias**. It was completed in an incredibly short time: the Parthenon itself took only ten years to finish.

The monuments survived barely altered for close to a thousand years, until in the reign of Emperor Justinian the temples were converted to **Christian** places of worship. Over the following centuries, the uses became secular as well as religious, and embellishments increased, gradually obscuring the Classical designs. Fifteenth-century Italian princes held court in the Propylaia, and the same quarters were later used by the **Turks** as their commander's headquarters and as a powder magazine. The Parthenon underwent similar changes from Greek to Roman temple, from Byzantine church to Frankish cathedral, before several centuries of use as a Turkish mosque. The Erechtheion, with its graceful female figures, saw service as a harem.

The Acropolis buildings finally fell victim to war, blown up during successive attempts by the Venetians to oust the Turks. In 1684 the Turks demolished the Temple of Athena Nike to gain a brief tactical advantage. Three years later the Venetians, laying siege to the hill, ignited a Turkish gunpowder magazine in the Parthenon, in the process blasting off its roof and starting a fire that raged for two days and nights.

The process of stripping down to the bare ruins seen today was completed by souvenir hunters and the efforts of the first archeologists (see p.56).

elegant, the Temple of Athena Nike stands on a precipitous platform overlooking the port of Pireás and the Saronic Gulf. Or at least it did. Prior to the Olympics the entire structure was dismantled, its pieces taken away for restoration and cleaning. It is still in the process of being rebuilt. Amazingly, this is not the first time this has happened: the Turks demolished the building in the seventeenth century, using it as material for a gun emplacement. Two hundred years later the temple was reconstructed from its original blocks.

In myth, it was from the platform beside the temple that King Aegeus maintained a vigil for the safe return of his son Theseus from his mission to slay the Minotaur on Crete. Theseus, flushed with success, forgot his promise to swap the boat's black sails for white on his return. Seeing the black sails, Aegeus assumed his son had perished and, racked with grief, threw himself to his death.

Some of the best views of the temple (when it's there) are from inside the Acropolis, to the right after passing through the Propylaia. Here also are the

A scaffolder's dream

If you see a photo of a pristine Parthenon standing against a clear sky, it is almost certainly an old one. For most of the twenty-first century the Acropolis buildings have been swathed in scaffolding and surrounded by cranes – at times some structures have even been removed altogether, to be cleaned and later replaced. Though originally intended to be complete in time for the 2004 Olympics, the work is now set to continue for the foreseeable future – some claim that it will be forty years before the job is complete.

There is little doubt that restoration was needed. Almost as soon as the War of Independence was over, Greek archeologists began clearing the Turkish village that had developed around the Parthenon-mosque, and much of their work was unintentionally destructive: the iron clamps and supports used to reinforce the marble structures, for example, have rusted and warped, causing the stones to crack. Meanwhile, earthquakes have dislodged the foundations, generations of feet have slowly worn down surfaces and, more recently, pollution has been turning the exposed marble to dust.

In 1975 the imminent collapse of the Parthenon was predicted and visitors have been barred from going inside any of the Acropolis buildings ever since. The restoration process includes – among many other things – replacing the iron clamps with titanium ones and removing many of the original friezes to the safety of museums, to be replaced by moulds. This work is aimed at ensuring that the Parthenon and its neighbours will continue to stand for another millenium or two but, in the meantime, it's not improving the view.

scant remains of a Sanctuary of Artemis. Although its function remains obscure, it is known that the precinct once housed a colossal bronze representation of the Wooden Horse of Troy. More noticeable is a nearby stretch of Mycenaean wall (running parallel to the Propylaia) that was incorporated into the Classical design.

The Parthenon

Main Acropolis site. The Parthenon was the first great building in Pericles' scheme, intended as a new sanctuary for Athena and a home for her cult image – a colossal wooden statue of Athena Polias (Athena of the City) overlaid with ivory and gold plating, with precious gems as eyes and an ivory gorgon death's-head on her breast. The sculpture has long been lost, but numerous later copies exist (including a fine Roman one

in the National Archeological Museum). Despite the statue, the Parthenon never rivalled the Erechtheion in sanctity, and its role tended to remain that of treasury and artistic showcase.

Originally the Parthenon's columns were brightly painted and it was decorated with the finest sculpture of the Classical age, depicting the Panathenaic procession, the birth of Athena and the struggles of Greeks to overcome giants, Amazons and centaurs – also brightly coloured. Of these, the best surviving examples are in the British Museum in London (see box, opposite); the Acropolis Museum has others, but the greater part of the pediments, along with the central columns and the cella, were destroyed by the Venetian bombardment in 1687.

To achieve the Parthenon's exceptional harmony of design,

its architect, Iktinos, used every trick known to the Doric order of architecture. Every ratio – length to width, width to height, and even such relationships as the distances between the columns and their diameter – is constant, while any possible appearance of disproportion is corrected by meticulous mathematics and craftsmanship.

▲ PARTHENON FRIEZE

The Erechtheion

Main Acropolis site. The Erechtheion, the last of the great works of Pericles to be completed, was the most revered of the ancient temples, built over sanctuaries predated by a Mycenaean palace. Both Athena and the city's old patron, Poseidon (known here as Erechtheus), were worshipped here. The site, according to myth, was that on which Athena and Poseidon held a contest, judged by their fellow Olympian gods, to determine who would possess Athens. At the touch of Athena's spear, the first-ever olive tree sprang from the ground, while Poseidon summoned forth a fountain of sea water. Athena won, and became patron of the city.

The Parthenon Marbles

The controversy over the so-called Elgin Marbles has its origin in the activities of Western looters at the start of the nineteenth century: above all the French ambassador Fauvel, gathering antiquities for the Louvre, and **Lord Elgin** levering away sculptures from the Parthenon. As British ambassador, Elgin obtained permission from the Turks to erect scaffolding, excavate and remove stones with inscriptions. He interpreted this concession as a licence to make off with almost all of the bas-reliefs from the Parthenon's frieze, most of its pedimental structures and a caryatid from the Erechtheion – all of which he later sold to the British Museum. While there were perhaps justifications for Elgin's action at the time – not least the Turks' tendency to use Parthenon stones in their lime kilns – his pilfering was controversial even then. Byron, for example, who visited in 1810–11 just in time to see the last of Elgin's ships loaded, roundly disparaged all this activity.

The Greeks hope that the long-awaited completion of the new Acropolis Museum (see p.60) will create the perfect opportunity for the British Museum to bow to pressure and return the marbles. But despite a campaign begun by Greek actress and culture minister Melina Mercouri in the early 1980s, there is so far little sign of that happening.

Today, the sacred objects within are long gone, but the series of elegant Ionic porticoes survive, the north one with a particularly fine decorated doorway and blue marble frieze. By far the most striking feature, however, is the famous Porch of the Caryatids, whose columns form the tunics of six tall maidens. The ones *in situ* are, sadly, replacements. Five of the originals are in the Acropolis Museum, while a sixth was looted by Elgin, who also removed a column and other purely architectural features – they're replaced here by casts in a different-colour marble.

The Acropolis Museum

Main Acropolis site. April–Sept Mon 11am–7pm, Tues–Sun 8am–7pm; Oct–March Mon 10am–3pm, Tues–Sun 8.30am–3pm. Placed discreetly on a level below that of the main monuments, the Acropolis Museum contains most of the important objects removed from the site since 1834. With new excavation the place has become much too small, and the whole collection should be moved soon to a dramatic new building below the Acropolis (see p.60). If you want more detail, museum guides are on sale, though it's also easy to eavesdrop on the many tour guides passing through – indeed usually it's impossible to avoid doing so.

In the first rooms, to the left as you enter, are fragments of sculptures from the old Temple of Athena (seventh to sixth century BC), whose traces of paint give a good indication of the vivid colours that were used in temple decoration. Further on is the Moschophoros, a painted marble statue of a young man carrying a sacrificial calf, dated 570 BC and one of the earliest examples of Greek art in marble. Room 4 displays one of the chief treasures of the building, a unique collection of Korai, or statues of maidens. The progression in style, from the simply contoured Doric clothing to the more elegant and voluminous Ionic designs, is fascinating; the figures' smiles also change subtly, becoming increasingly loose and natural.

The pieces of the Parthenon frieze in Room 8 were buried in the explosion that destroyed the Parthenon, thereby escaping the clutches of Lord Elgin. This room also contains a graceful and fluid sculpture, known as *Iy Sandalízoussa*, which depicts Athena Nike adjusting her sandal. Finally, in the last room are four authentic and semi-eroded caryatids from the Erechtheion, displayed behind a glass screen in a carefully rarefied atmosphere.

▼ ACROPOLIS MUSEUM

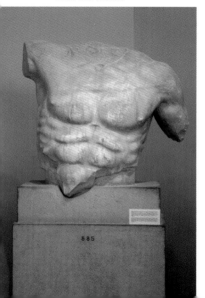

885

▲ THEATRE OF DIONYSOS

Theatre of Dionysos

South Slope site. The Theatre of Dionysos is one of the most evocative locations in the city. Here the masterpieces of Aeschylus, Sophocles, Euripides and Aristophanes were first performed; it was also the venue in Classical times for the annual festival of tragic drama, where each Greek citizen would take his turn as member of the chorus. Rebuilt in the fourth century BC, the theatre could hold some 17,000 spectators – considerably more than Herodes Atticus's 5000–6000 seats; twenty of the original 64 tiers of seats survive. Most notable are the great marble thrones in the front row, each inscribed with the name of an official of the festival or of an important priest; in the middle sat the priest of Dionysos and on his right the representative of the Delphic Oracle. At the rear of the stage are reliefs of episodes in the life of Dionysos. Sadly, this area is roped off to protect the stage-floor mosaic, a magnificent diamond of multicoloured marble best seen from the seats above.

Around the Theatre

South Slope site. The dominant structure on the south side of the Acropolis – much more immediately obvious even than the Theatre of Dionysos – is the second-century Roman Herodes Atticus Theatre (Odeion of Herodes Atticus). This has been extensively restored for performances of music and Classical drama during the summer festival (see p.183). Unfortunately, it's open only for shows; at other times you'll have to be content with spying over the wall.

Between the two theatres lie the foundations of the Stoa of Eumenes, originally a massive colonnade of stalls erected in the second century BC. Above the stoa, high up under the walls of the Acropolis, extend the ruins of the Asklepion, a sanctuary devoted to the healing god Asklepios and built around a sacred spring. Like much of the surrounding area, this is being restored, and there are extensive new signs in English. Nearby, above the Theatre of Dionysos, you can see the entry to a huge cave. This housed the Choregic Monument of Thrasyllos, and its entrance was closed off around 320 BC with a marble facade – this too is currently being restored. The cave was later converted to Christian use and became the chapel of Virgin Mary of the Rocks, but an ancient statue of Dionysos remained inside until it was removed by Lord Elgin (it's now in the British Museum), while the Classical structure survived almost unchanged until 1827, when it was blown up in a Turkish siege.

The New Acropolis Museum

Leóforos Dhionysíou Areopayítou, opposite the South Slope site. After years of delays, work on the huge new Acropolis Museum finally began in 2003. This is set to be stunning: the top storey is an all-glass affair designed to house the Parthenon Marbles (those already in the Acropolis Museum, plus the restored Elgin Marbles), with a direct view up to the Parthenon itself. Downstairs, the rest of the contents of the current Acropolis Museum will be far better displayed than they can be now, and there's also a raised, part-glass floor added to the design, to preserve and display remains of early Christian Athens discovered during building work.

The Areopagus

Immediately below the entrance to the Acropolis. Metal steps as well as ancient, slippery, rock-hewn stairs ascend the low, unfenced hill of the Areopagus. The "Hill of Ares" was the site of

the Council of Nobles and the Judicial Court under the aristocratic rule of ancient Athens. During the Classical period the court lost its powers of government to the Assembly (held on the Pnyx) but it remained the court of criminal justice, dealing primarily with cases of homicide.

In myth, it was also the site where Ares, God of War, was tried for the murder of one of Poseidon's sons; Aeschylus used the setting in *The Eumenides* for the trial of Orestes, who, pursued by the Furies' demand of "a life for a life", stood accused of murdering his mother Clytemnestra. The Persians camped here during their siege of the Acropolis in 480 BC, and in the Roman era St Paul preached the "Sermon on an Unknown God" on the hill, winning amongst his converts Dionysios "the Areopagite", who became the city's patron saint.

Today, there's little evidence of ancient grandeur, and the hill is littered with cigarette butts and empty beer-cans left by the crowds who come to rest after their exertions on the Acropolis and to enjoy the views. These, at least, are good – down over the Agora and towards the ancient cemetery of Kerameikos.

The Ancient Agora

Ancient Agora site. The Agora or market was the heart of ancient Athenian city life from as early as 3000 BC. Today, the site is an extensive and rather confusing jumble of ruins, dating from various stages of building between the sixth century BC and the fifth century AD. As well as the marketplace, the Agora was the chief meeting-place of the city, where orators held forth, business was discussed and gossip exchanged. It was also the first home of the democratic assembly before that shifted to the Pnyx, and continued to be its meeting place when cases of ostracism were discussed for most of the Classical period.

Originally the Agora was a rectangle, divided diagonally by the Panathenaic Way and enclosed by temples, administrative buildings, and long porticoed *stoas* (arcades of shops). In the centre was an open space, defined by boundary stones.

The best overview of the site is from the exceptionally well-preserved Hephaisteion, or **Temple of Hephaistos**, which overlooks the rest of the site from the west. An observation point in front of it has a plan showing the buildings as they were in 150 AD, and the various remains laid out in front of you make a lot more sense with this to help (there are similar plans at the entrances, and upstairs in the Stoa of Attalos). The temple itself was originally thought to be dedicated to Theseus, because his exploits are depicted on the frieze (hence Thissíon, which has given its name to the area); more recently it has been accepted that it actually honoured Hephaistos, patron of blacksmiths and metal-workers. It was one of the earliest buildings of Pericles' programme, but also one of the

▼ STOA OF ATTALOS

least known – perhaps because it lacks the curvature and "lightness" of the Parthenon's design. The barrel-vaulted roof dates from a Byzantine conversion into the church of St George.

The other church on the site – that of Áyii Apóstoli (the Holy Apostles), by the south entrance – is worth a look as you wander among the extensive foundations of the other Agora buildings. Inside are fragments of fresco, exposed during restoration of the eleventh-century shrine.

Stoa of Attalos

Ancient Agora site. Same hours as Agora (see box, p.53) but opens 11am Mon; upper floor Mon–Fri 9am–2.30pm. For some background to the Agora, head for the Stoa of Attalos. Originally constructed around 158 BC, the Stoa was completely rebuilt between 1953 and 1956 and is, in every respect except colour, an entirely faithful reconstruction; lacking its original bright red and blue paint or no, it is undeniably spectacular.

A small museum occupies ten of the 21 shops that formed the lower level of the building. It displays items found at the Agora site from the earliest Neolithic occupation to Roman and Byzantine times. Many of the early items come from burials, but as ever the highlights are from the Classical era, including some good red-figure pottery and a bronze Spartan shield. Look out for the ostraka, or shards of pottery, with names written on them. At annual assemblies of the citizens, these ostraka would be handed in, and the individual with most votes banished, or "ostracized", from the city for ten years.

On the upper level, the balcony area has a sparse but fascinating little exhibition on the excavations of the Agora site and reconstruction of the Stoa, with various models, plans and photos of buildings. The models especially help make sense of the rest of the Agora site.

Pláka

The largely pedestrianized area of Pláka, with its narrow lanes and stepped alleys climbing towards the Acropolis, is arguably the most attractive part of Athens, and certainly the most popular with visitors. In addition to a scattering of ancient sites and various offbeat and enjoyable museums, it offers glimpses of an older Athens, refreshingly at odds with the concrete blocks of the metropolis.

Although surrounded by huge, traffic-choked avenues, Pláka itself is a welcome escape, its narrow streets offering no through-routes for traffic even where you are allowed to drive. Nineteenth-century houses, some grand, some humble, can be seen everywhere, their gateways opening onto verdant courtyards overlooked by wooden verandahs. With scores of cafés and restaurants to fill the time between museums and sites, and streets lined with touristy shops, it's an enjoyable place to wander. The main disadvantage is price – things are noticeably more expensive in Pláka than in much of the rest of the city.

Museum of Greek Folk Art

Kydhathinéon 17. Tues–Sun 9am–2pm. €2. The Folk Art Museum is one of the most enjoyable in the city, even though let down somewhat by poor lighting and labelling. Its five floors are devoted to displays of weaving, pottery, regional costumes and embroidery, along with other traditional Greek arts and crafts. On the mezzanine floor, the carnival tradition of northern Greece and the all-but-vanished shadow-puppet theatre are featured. The second floor features exhibits of gold and silver jewellery and weaponry, much of it from the era of the War of Independence. The highlight, though, is on the first floor: the reconstructed room from a house on the island of Lesvós with a series of wonderful murals by the primitive artist Theofilos (1868–1934) displaying naive scenes from Greek folklore and history, especially the independence struggle.

▼ SHOPS ON ADHRIANOÚ

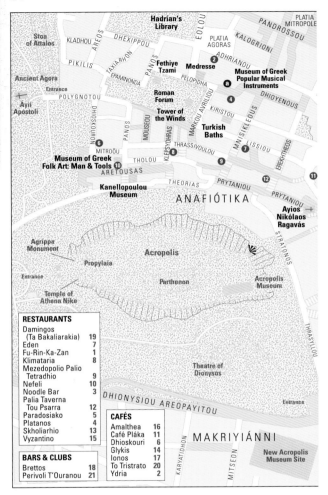

RESTAURANTS

Damingos
(Ta Bakaliarakia) **19**
Eden **7**
Fu-Rin-Ka-Zan **1**
Klimataria **8**
Mezedopolio Palio
Tetradhio **9**
Nefeli **10**
Noodle Bar **3**
Palia Taverna
Tou Psarra **12**
Paradosiako **5**
Platanos **4**
Skholiarhio **13**
Vyzantino **15**

BARS & CLUBS

Brettos **18**
Perivoli T'Ouranou **21**

CAFÉS

Amalthea **16**
Café Pláka **11**
Dhioskouri **6**
Glykis **14**
Ionos **17**
To Tristato **20**
Ydria **2**

Children's Museum

Kydhathinéon 14. Tues–Fri 10am–2pm, Sat & Sun 10am–3pm. Free. Aimed at the under-12s, the Children's Museum is as much a play area as a museum. Labelling is entirely in Greek, and the place is primarily geared to school groups, who take part in activities such as chocolate-making – but it should keep young kids amused for a while. Permanent exhibits include features on the Athens metro, how computers work, and the human body.

Frissiras Museum

Monis Asteríou 3 and 7 ⓦwww .frissirasmuseum.com. Wed–Fri 10am–5pm, Sat & Sun 11am–5pm. €6. Housed in two beautifully

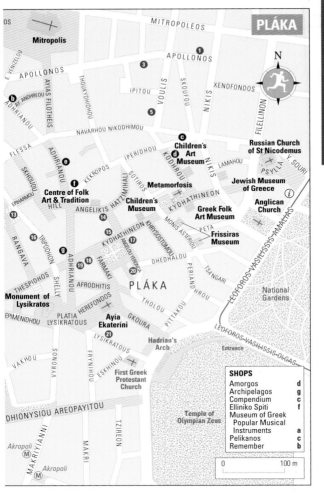

SHOPS

Amorgos	**d**
Archipelagos	**g**
Compendium	**c**
Elliniko Spiti	**f**
Museum of Greek Popular Musical Instruments	**a**
Pelikanos	**c**
Remember	**b**

renovated Neoclassical buildings, the Frissiras Museum is billed as Greece's only museum of contemporary European art. It has over three thousand works – mostly figurative painting plus a few sculptures, a regular programme of exhibitions, a fine shop and an elegant café. The space at no. 7 houses the permanent exhibition, which includes plenty of names familiar to English-speakers – David Hockney, Peter Blake, Paula Rego among them – as well as many lesser-known Greek and other European artists. Temporary exhibitions, along with the shop and café, are at no. 3 a block away.

Centre of Folk Art and Tradition

Angelikís Hatzimiháli 6. Tues–Fri 9am–1pm & 5–9pm, Sat & Sun 9am–1pm. Free. The Centre of Folk Art and Tradition houses a collection of costumes, embroidery, lace and weaving, along with musical instruments, ceramics, and icons and religious artefacts. It occupies the former home of Angelikís Hatzimiháli, whose championing of traditional Greek arts and crafts was one of the chief catalysts for their revival in the early twentieth century. The house itself – designed for her in the 1920s in a Greek Art-Nouveau or Arts & Crafts style – is a large part of the attraction, with its cool, high rooms and finely carved wooden doors, windows and staircase. At the back, narrow stairs descend to the kitchen with its original range, while upstairs there's a library and rooms where classes are held to pass on the traditions of crafts like embroidery and weaving.

Jewish Museum of Greece

Níkis 39. ⊛www.jewishmuseum.gr. Mon–Fri 9am–2.30pm, Sun 10am–2pm. €5. Elegantly presented in a series of dimly lit rooms, with plenty of explanation in English, the Jewish Museum tells the history of Jews in Greece. Downstairs are art and religious paraphernalia, many of the pieces centuries old. The centrepiece is the reconstructed synagogue of Pátra, dating from the 1920s, whose furnishings have been moved here en bloc and remounted.

Upstairs, more recent history includes World War II and the German occupation, when Greece's Jewish population was reduced from almost 80,000 to less than 10,000. There are features, too, on the part played by Jews in the Greek resistance, and stories of survival.

Museum of Greek Children's Art

Kódhrou 9. ⊛www.childrensart-museum.gr. Tues–Sat 10am–2pm, Sun 11am–2pm; closed Aug. €2. The Children's Art Museum does exactly what it says on the label – displays art by Greek children. There are a few permanent exhibits, but mainly the works are the winning entries to an annual nationwide art contest open to children up to the age of 14. On the whole, it is wonderfully uplifting.

The Monument of Lysikratos

In the southeastern corner of Pláka, the Monument of Lysikratos, a graceful stone and marble structure from 335 BC, rises from a small, triangular open area overlooked by a quiet café/taverna. It's near the end of Odhós Tripódhon, a relic of the ancient Street of the Tripods, where winners of drama competitions erected monuments to dedicate their trophies (in the form of tripod cauldrons) to Dionysos. The Monument of Lysikratos is the only survivor of these triumphal memorials. A four-metre-high stone base supports six Corinthian columns rising up to a marble dome on which, in a flourish of acanthus-leaf carvings, the winning tripod was placed. The inscription tells us that "Lysikratos of Kikyna, son of Lysitheides, was *choregos* (sponsor); the tribe of Akamantis won the victory with a chorus of boys; Theon played the flute; Lysiades of Athens trained the chorus; Evainetos was archon.".

▲ MONUMENT OF LYSIKRATOS

In the seventeenth century the monument became part of a Capuchin convent, which provided regular lodgings for European travellers – Byron is said to have written part of *Childe Harold* here, and the street beyond, Výronos, is named after him. The old Street of the Tripods would have continued in this direction – many important ancient Athenian buildings are thought to lie undiscovered in the vicinity.

Ayía Ekateríni Church

Platía Ayía Ekateríni. Mon–Fri 7.30am–12.30pm & 5–6.30pm, Sat & Sun 5–10pm. Free. St Catherine's Church is one of the few in Pláka that's routinely open. At its heart is an eleventh-century Byzantine original – although it has been pretty well hidden by later additions. You can see it most clearly from the back of the church, while in the courtyard in front are foundations of a Roman building. Inside, the over-restored frescoes look brand new, and there are plenty of glittering icons.

Kanellopoulou Museum

Theorías 12, cnr Panós. Tues–Sun 8.30am–3pm. €2. Though there's nothing here that you won't see examples of in the bigger museums, the Kanellopoulou collection, exhibited in the topmost house under the Acropolis, is well worth a visit. On the lower floors the many gorgeous gilded icons first grab your attention, but there's also Byzantine jewellery, bronze oil-lamps and crosses, and Roman funerary ornaments; some of the smaller items are exquisite.

The Anafiótika

The main arteries of Pláka, above all marble-paved **Kydhathinéon** with its crowds of restaurants and **Adhrianoú**, home of the Manchester United beach towel and "Sex in Ancient Greece" playing cards, can become depressingly touristy. For a break, climb up into the jumble of streets and alleys that cling to the lower slopes of the Acropolis. Here, the whitewashed, island-style houses and ancient churches of the **Anafiótika** quarter proclaim a cheerfully architect-free zone. There's still the odd shop, and taverna tables are set out wherever a bit of flat ground can be found, but there are also plenty of hidden corners redolent of a quieter era.

Upstairs is ancient pottery and bronze, including items from Minoan Crete and from Egypt, and Stone Age tools. The top floor is perhaps the best of all, with pottery and gold jewellery from the Geometric, Classical, Hellenistic and Roman periods. Items here range from some astonishingly well-preserved large water jars and kraters to the bronze ram from the prow of a battleship, shaped like a dog's snout.

Museum of Greek Folk Art: Man and Tools

Panós 22. Tues–Sat 9am–2.30pm. €2. A new branch of the Greek Folk Art museum, set in another fine mansion, this is devoted to the world of work. Tiny but fascinating and with good English labelling, its exhibits of tools and antiquated machinery concentrate on the pre-industrial world: there's a wooden grape-press as well as tools used in traditional trades including agriculture, barrel-making, cobbling and metalwork.

Roman Forum

Entrance at Pelopídha, cnr Eólou. Daily: April–Sept 8am–7.30pm; Oct–March 8.30am–3pm. €2 or joint Acropolis ticket. The Roman Forum was built during the reign of Julius Caesar and his successor Augustus as an extension of the older ancient Greek agora. Its main entrance was on the west side, through the Gate of Athena Archegetis, which, along with the Tower of the Winds (see opposite), is still the most prominent remain on the site. This gate marked the end of a street leading up from the Greek agora, and its four surviving columns give a vivid impression of the grandeur of the original portal. On the side facing the Acropolis you can still make out an engraved edict of Hadrian announcing the rules and taxes on the sale of oil. On the opposite side of the Forum, a second gateway is also easily made out, and between the

Roman Athens

In 146 BC the **Romans** ousted Athens' Macedonian rulers and incorporated the city into their vast new province of Achaia. The city's status as a renowned seat of learning and great artistic centre ensured that it was treated with respect, and Athenian artists and architects were much in demand in Rome. Not much changed, in fact: there were few major construction projects, and what building there was tended to follow Classical Greek patterns.

The **history** of this period was shaped for the most part by the city's alliances, which often proved unfortunate. In 86 BC, for example, Sulla punished Athens for its allegiance to his rival Mithridates by burning its fortifications and looting its treasures. His successors were more lenient; Julius Caesar offered a free pardon after Athens had sided with Pompey, and Octavian (Augustus) showed similar clemency when Athens harboured Brutus following Caesar's assassination.

The one Roman emperor who did spend a significant amount of time in Athens, and left his mark here, was **Hadrian** (reigned 117–138 AD). Among his grandiose monuments are Hadrian's Arch, a magnificent and immense library and (though it had been begun centuries before) the Temple of Olympian Zeus. A generation later, **Herodes Atticus**, a Roman senator who owned extensive lands in Marathon, became the city's last major benefactor of ancient times.

two is the marketplace itself, surrounded by colonnades and shops, some of which have been excavated. Inside the fenced site, but just outside the market area to the east, are the foundations of public latrines dating from the first century AD.

The Tower of the Winds

Roman Forum. The best preserved and easily the most intriguing of the ruins inside the Forum site is the graceful octagonal structure known as the Tower of the Winds. This predates the Forum, and stands just outside the main market area. Designed in the first century BC by Andronikos of Kyrrhos, a Syrian astronomer, it served as a compass, sundial, weather vane and water clock – the last powered by a stream from one of the Acropolis springs.

Each face of the tower is adorned with a relief of a figure floating through the air, personifying the eight winds. Beneath each of these it is still possible to make out the markings of eight sundials. The semicircular tower attached to the south face was the reservoir from which water was channelled into a cylinder in the main tower; the time was read by the water level viewed through the open northwest door. On the top of the building was a bronze weather vane in the form of the sea god, Triton. In Ottoman times, dervishes used the tower as a *tekke* or ceremonial hall, terrifying their superstitious Orthodox neighbours with their chanting, music and whirling meditation.

Fethiye Tzami and the medresse

In the area around the Roman Forum can be seen some of the few visible reminders of the Ottoman city. The oldest mosque in Athens, the Fethiye Tzami, built in 1458, actually occupies a corner of the Forum site. It was dedicated by Sultan Mehmet II, who conquered Constantinople in 1453 (*fethiye* means "conquest" in Turkish). There's a fine, porticoed entrance, but sadly, you can't see inside, as it's now used as an archeological warehouse.

Across Eólou from here, more or less opposite the Forum entrance, the gateway and single dome of a **medresse**, an Islamic school, survive. During the last years of Ottoman rule and the early years of Greek independence, this was used as a prison and was notorious for its bad conditions; a plane tree in the courtyard was used for hangings. The prison was closed in the 1900s and most of the building torn down.

Turkish Baths

Kiristou 8. Mon & Wed–Sun 9am–2.30pm. €2. Constructed originally in the 1450s, the Turkish baths were in use, with many later additions, right up to 1965. Newly restored, they now offer an insight into a part of Athens' past that is rarely glimpsed and well worth a look. Traditionally, the baths would have been used in shifts by men and women, although expansion in the nineteenth century provided the separate facilities you see today. The tepidarium and caldarium, fitted out in marble with domed roofs and rooflights, are particularly beautiful. The underfloor and wall heating systems have been exposed in places, while upstairs there are photos and pictures of old Athens. Labelling throughout is in Greek only,

▲ TURKISH BATHS

so it may be worth using the audio tour on offer (€1, plus a deposit).

Museum of Greek Popular Musical Instruments

Dhioyénous 1–3. Tues–Sun 10am–2pm. Free. Superbly displayed in the rooms of a Neoclassical building, the Museum of Greek Popular Musical Instruments traces the history of virtually every type of musical instrument that has ever been played in Greece. There are drums and wind instruments of all sorts (from crude bagpipes to clarinets) on the ground floor, lyras, fiddles, lutes and a profusion of stringed instruments upstairs. In the basement there are more percussion and toy instruments including some not-so-obvious festival and liturgical items such as triangles, strikers, livestock bells along with carnival outfits.

Reproductions of frescoes show the Byzantine antecedents of many instruments, and headphone sets are provided for sampling the music made by the various exhibits.

The museum shop has an excellent selection of CDs for sale, concentrating, not surprisingly, on traditional Greek music.

Shops

Amorgos

Kódhrou 3. A small shop filled with an eclectic collection of tasteful woodcarvings, needlework, lamps, lace, shadow puppets and other handicrafts.

Archipelagos

Adhrianoú 142. Handmade jewellery and ceramics. A small, inviting boutique with exquisite designs on a Greek theme. Adjustments can be made while you wait.

Compendium

Nikodhímou 5, cnr Iperídhou. Long-established English-language bookshop: small secondhand section, noticeboards for travellers and residents, and regular poetry readings and other events.

Elliniko Spiti

Kekropós 14, just off Adhrianoú. Amazing artworks and pieces of furniture created from found materials, especially driftwood but also metal and marble. Probably too big to take home (for your wallet as well as your suitcase), but well worth a look.

Museum of Greek Popular Musical Instruments

Dhioyénous 1–3. Excellent selection of CDs of traditional Greek music, albeit not cheap, plus some simple musical instruments if you want to try your hand at playing it yourself.

Pelikanos

Adhrianoú 115. Tiny shop specializing in copper and brassware, a mix of old pieces as well as new ones that George Pelikanos makes himself.

Remember

Adhrianoú 79. Dimitris Tsouanato's shop has been around for 25 years but never seems to run out of inspiration: if there is one piece of clothing you should buy in Athens it's one of his hand-painted T-shirts. Also stocks rock memorabilia and has some amazing sculptures in the courtyard.

Cafés

Amalthea

Tripódhon 16. Tasteful if pricey café-patisserie, serving yoghurt and crêpes as well as non-alcoholic drinks.

Café Pláka

Tripódhon 1. Touristy but convenient – offers crêpes, sandwiches, ice cream and a roof terrace on which to enjoy them.

Dhioskouri

Dhioskoúron, cnr Mitröon. Popular café right on the edge of Pláka overlooking the Agora. Simple food – salads and omelettes – as well as the inevitable frappés and cappuccinos.

Glykis

Angélou Yéronda 2. A secluded corner under shaded trees just off busy Kydhathinéon, frequented by a young Greek crowd. It has a mouthwatering array of sweets, as well as cold and hot appetizer plates.

Ionos

Angélou Yéronda 7. Good coffees and snacks, but above all a great place to people-watch on the busy Platía Filomoússou Eterías.

To Tristrato

Dhedhálou 34, cnr Angélou Yéronda. Daily 2pm–midnight. Lovely little traditional-style café

PLACES

Pláka

▼ OLD HOUSES AGAINST ACROPOLIS WALLS

▲ PLÁKA ALLEYWAY

just off the madness of Platía Filomoússou Eterías: coffee, juices, sandwiches, desserts and cakes.

Ydria

Adhrianoú 68, cnr Eólou. Platía Paliás Agorás, just round the corner from the Roman Forum, is packed with the tables of competing cafés: this is one of the best. A lovely place to sit outside for a quiet coffee or breakfast (they also serve more substantial meals), though, like its neighbours, very expensive.

Restaurants

Byzantino

Kydhathinéon 18, on Platía Filomoússou Eterías ☏ 210 32 27 368. Reliable, traditional taverna that still attracts locals on this busy, touristy square. Take a look in the kitchen at the moderately priced daily specials, such as stuffed tomatoes or *youvétsi*.

Damingos (Ta Bakaliarakia)

Kydhathinéon 41 ☏ 210 32 25 084. Eves only; closed mid-July to end Aug. Tucked away in a basement since 1865, this place has dour service, but the old-fashioned style (hefty barrels in the back room filled with the family's home vintages including a memorable *retsina*), and the excellent *bakaliáro skordhaliá* (cod with garlic sauce) for which it is famed (and named) make up for it.

Eden

Lissiou 12, off Mnisikléous ☏ 210 32 48 858. Closed Tues. Vegetarian restaurant in a nineteenth-century mansion with a somewhat formal atmosphere. Seating is indoors only and there have been some complaints of small portions and high prices; the food is good, though, with plenty of things you won't often see in Greece such as mushroom pie, chilli, and soya lasagna.

Fu-Rin-Ka-Zan

Apóllonos 2 ☏ 210 32 29 170. Closed Sun. Busy Japanese restaurant – popular at lunchtimes – with sushi, sashimi, yakisoba and the like at reasonable prices.

Klimataria

Klepsýdhras 5 ☏ 210 32 11 215. Eves only. Over a hundred years old, this unpretentious, pleasant taverna serves simple food – mainly grilled meat and fish. In winter, you're likely to be treated to live music, which inspires sing-alongs by the mostly Greek clientele.

▲ BYZANTINO

Mezedopolio Palio Tetradhio

Mnisikléous 26, cnr Thrassívoulou, Pláka ☎210 32 11 903. One of the touristy tavernas with tables set out on the stepped streets beneath the Acropolis. The food is a cut above that of most of its neighbours, though you pay for the romantic setting. Live music some evenings.

Nefeli

Pános 24, cnr Aretoúsas ☎210 32 12 475. Taverna eves only, Ouzerí open all day. Delightful setting on a peaceful side-street, with tables outside under a secluded grape arbour or in an old mansion with a panoramic view. Serves a small but interesting selection of moderately priced classic Greek dishes such as veal and lamb *stamna* (casserole baked in a clay pot). There's live Greek music (Fri, Sat & Sun nights) and a small dance-floor. The adjacent synonymous ouzerí, overlooking the church of Ayía Anna, is a busier local hangout favoured by young Greeks.

Noodle Bar

Apóllonos 11 ☎210 33 18 585. Fairly basic and inexpensive place (takeaway too) serving decent Asian food – Thai predominantly but also with Indian, Chinese and Indonesian flavours.

Palia Taverna Tou Psarra

Erekhthéos 16 at Erotókritou ☎210 32 18 733. Large, classic Greek

▼ TAVERNA IN PLÁKA

▲ PALIA TAVERNA TOU PSARRA, PLÁKA

taverna around a restored old mansion with plenty of tables outside, on a tree-shaded and bougainvillea-draped pedestrian crossroads. You're best making a meal of the *mezédhes*, which include humble standards as well as seafood and fish concoctions.

Paradosiako

Voulís 44a, Pláka ☎210 32 14 121. Small place on a busy street serving unpretentious, reasonably priced, fresh Greek food.

Platanos

Dhioyénous 4 ☎210 32 20 666. A long-established taverna, with outdoor summer seating in a quiet square under the plane tree from which it takes its name. Good-value traditional dishes such as chops and roast lamb with artichokes or spinach and potatoes, and quaffable house wine from vast barrels.

Skholiarhio

Tripódhon 14 ☎210 32 47 605, ⓦwww.sholarhio.gr. Daily 11am–2am. Attractive split-level taverna, known as *Kouklis* by the locals, with a perennially popular summer terrace, sheltered from the street. It has a great selection of *mezédhes* (all €2–4) brought out on long trays so that you can point to the ones you fancy. Especially good are the flaming sausages, *bouréki* (thin pastry filled with ham and cheese) and grilled aubergine. The house red wine is also palatable and cheap. All-

▼ SKHOLIARHIO TAVERNA

▲ BRETTOS

inclusive deals for larger groups at around €10 a head.

Bars & clubs

Brettos

Kydhathinéon 41 ☏ 210 32 32 110. By day a liquor store, selling mainly the products of their own family distillery, at night *Brettos* is one of the few bars in Pláka. It's a simple, unpretentious place with barrels along one wall and a huge range of bottles, backlit at night, along another.

Perivoli T'Ouranou

Lysikrátous 19 ☏ 210 32 35 517. Closed summer months. Traditional rebétika club on the edge of Pláka (so used to tourists) with regular appearances by classy performer Babis Tsertsos.

Monastiráki and Psyrrí

Monastiráki and Psyrrí are enjoyable parts of Athens. Less touristy than Pláka to the south, there are nevertheless plenty of sights and extensive opportunities for eating, drinking and shopping. The Monastiráki area, fringing the Agora and Roman Forum and with the modern market on the other side, has been a commercial hub of the city since ancient times. Here the narrow lanes of Pláka start to open up, to the so-called Flea Market and streets that are noisier, busier and more geared to everyday living.

The traffic-free upper half of Odhós Ermoú, towards Sýndagma, is one of the city's prime shopping streets, full of familiar high-street chains and department stores: if you're after Zara or Marks & Spencer, Mothercare or Benetton, this is the place to head. In the other direction, in the western half of the Flea Market and across Ermoú towards Psyrrí, are some funkier alternatives, with interesting new designer and retro stores mixed in with jumbley antiques places.

This is also a great place to eat and drink: between them, Monastiráki and Psyrrí probably have more eating places per square foot than anywhere else in Athens. Their characters are quite different, though. Monastiráki restaurants tend to be simple and functional – especially the line of tavernas that spill onto Mitropóleos as it heads up from Platía Monastirakíou.

Psyrrí is more of a venue for an evening out – home to a throng of trendy restaurants, *mezedhopolía* and bars. Buzzing till late every evening, it doesn't have a great deal to offer by day, although the cafés seem to attract crowds whatever the time. Psyrrí's own website – ⓦ www.psirri.gr – is an excellent place to find out what's going on and lists virtually every restaurant, bar, shop and gallery in the area.

▼ HADRIAN'S LIBRARY

Hadrian's Library

Entrance on Áreos.
Daily 8am–3pm. Free.

Bordering the north end of the Roman Forum, and stretching right through from Áreos to Eólou, stand the surviving walls and columns of Hadrian's Library, an enormous building dating from 132 AD that enclosed a cloistered court of a hundred columns. Despite the name, this was much more than just a library – more a cultural centre including art galleries, lecture halls and a great public space at its centre. The site has only recently opened to the public and is still being excavated: for the moment remains are sparse and poorly labelled. Much of it has been built over many times, and a lot of what you can see today consists of the foundations and mosaic floors of later Byzantine churches. However, some of the original columns survive, and above all you get an excellent sense of the sheer scale of the original building, especially when you realize that the Tetraconch Church, whose remains lie at the centre of the site, was built entirely within the library's internal courtyard.

Museum of Greek Folk Art: Ceramics Collection

Áreos 1. Mon & Wed–Sun 9am–2.30pm. €2. Squeezed between the walls of Hadrian's Library and the shacks of Pandhróssou stands the Mosque of Tzisdarákis. Built in 1759, it has had a

▲ CERAMICS MUSEUM

chequered life – converted to a barracks and then a jail after Greek independence, before becoming the original home of the Greek Folk Art Museum in 1918. Today, as a branch of that museum, it houses the Kyriazópoulos collection of ceramics – the legacy of a Thessaloníki professor. Good as it is, the collection is in all honesty likely to excite you only if you have a particular interest in pottery; most people will probably find the building itself, the only one of Athens' old mosques whose interior can be seen, at least as big an attraction.

Though missing its minaret, and with a balcony added inside for the museum, plenty of original features remain. In the airy, domed space, look out for the striped *mihrab* (the niche indicating the direction of Mecca), a calligraphic inscription above the entrance

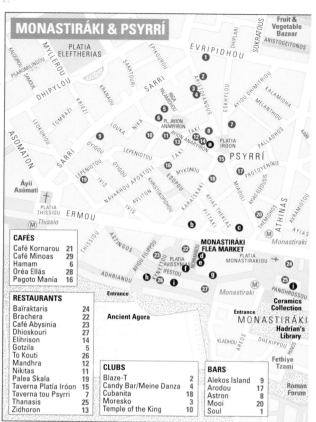

MONASTIRÁKI & PSYRRÍ

CAFÉS	
Café Kornarou	21
Café Minoas	29
Hamam	6
Oréa Ellás	28
Pagoto Manía	16

RESTAURANTS	
Baïraktaris	24
Brachera	22
Café Abysinia	23
Dhioskouri	27
Elihrison	14
Gotzila	5
To Kouti	26
Mandhra	12
Nikitas	11
Palea Skala	19
Taverna Platía Iróon	15
Taverna tou Psyrrí	7
Thanasis	25
Zidhoron	13

CLUBS	
Blaze-T	2
Candy Bar/Meine Danza	4
Cubanita	18
Moresko	3
Temple of the King	10

BARS	
Alekos Island	9
Arodou	17
Astron	8
Mooi	20
Soul	1

recording the mosque's founder and date, and a series of niches used as extra *mihrabs* for occasions when worshippers could not fit into the main hall.

Monastiráki Flea Market

Platía Monastirakíou gets its name from the little monastery church (*monastiráki*) at its centre. Full of fruit stalls, nut sellers, lottery vendors and kiosks, the square lies at the heart of an area that has been a marketplace since Ottoman times and still preserves, in places, a bazaar atmosphere.

In each direction you'll see signs proclaiming that you are entering the famous Monastiráki Flea Market. These days this is a bit of a misnomer – there's plenty of shopping, but mostly of a very conventional nature. To the east, Odhós Pandhróssou is almost entirely geared towards tourists.

West of Platía Monastiráki the flea market has more of its old character, and you'll find shops full of handmade musical instruments, or chess and *tavlí* boards, as well as places selling bikes, skateboards or camping gear. An alley off

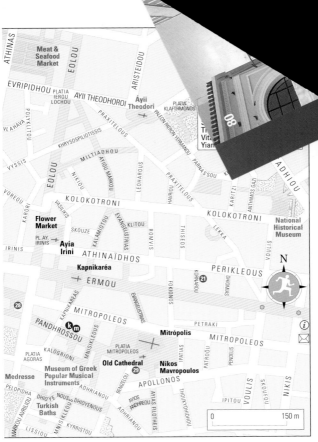

Iféstou is jammed with record and CD shops, with a huge basement secondhand bookshop. Around Normánou and **Platía Avyssinías** shops specialize in furniture and junky antiques: from here to Adhrianoú, the relics of the real flea market survive in hopeless jumble-sale rejects, touted by a cast of eccentrics (especially on Sundays). Odhós Adhrianoú is at its most appealing at this end, with a couple of interesting antique shops, and some shady cafés overlooking the metro lines, Agora and Acropolis.

The Kapnikaréa

Mon, Wed & Sat 8am–1pm, Tues, Thurs & Fri 8am–12.30pm & 5–7.30pm, Sun 8–11.30am. Free.

The pretty Byzantine church of Kapnikaréa marks more or less the beginning of the upmarket shopping on Ermoú, looking tiny in these high-rise urban surroundings. Originally eleventh century, but with later additions, it has a lovely little dome and a gloomy interior in which you can just about make out the modern frescoes. The church is allegedly named after its founder, a tax collector:

▲ FLEA MARKET

edifice; the old cathedral alongside it is dwarfed by comparison, but infinitely more attractive. There is said to have been a church on this site since the very earliest days of Christianity in Athens. What you see now dates from the twelfth century, a beautiful little structure cobbled together from plain and carved blocks from earlier incarnations – some almost certainly from that original church.

kapnós means smoke, and in the Byzantine era a tax on houses was known as the smoke tax.

Platía Mitropóleos

A welcome spot of calm among the busy shopping streets surrounding it, Platía Mitropóleos – Cathedral Square – is home to not just one but two cathedrals. The modern Mitrópolis is a large, clumsy nineteenth-century

Shops

2morrow

Kynéttou 3, in the Flea Market. Yota Kayaba sells her designs on the first floor of the building where she also creates them. A small collection of interesting vintage and ethnic clothes too.

7+7

Iféstou 7. A choice selection of old and new rock and Greek music on vinyl and CD. This alley in the Flea Market has several other record and secondhand-book stores.

▼ KAPNIKARÉA CHURCH

Annita Patrikiadhou

Pandhróssou 58. Short on atmosphere, but genuine antiquities – pottery and coins mainly, some of them made into jewellery – are sold here, with official export licences to guarantee authenticity and legality. Prices are steep, but then many of the items are over 2000 years old.

Athena's Sandals

Normánou 7 ⓦwww .melissinos-sandals.gr. Stavros Melissinos, the "poet sandal-maker", was an Athens institution, numbering The Beatles, Anthony Quinn and Sophia Loren amongst his hundreds of celebrity clients. Now retired, his daughter carries on his tradition here – with interesting leatherwork of all kinds alongside the sandals – while a son has a rival store nearby (see below).

Epidemic

Ayíon Anaryíron 5. Designer clothes for the young fashion-victims of Psyrrí.

Kendro Ellinikis Paradosis

Entrances at Mitropóleos 59 and Pandhróssou 36. As the name, "Centre of Hellenic Tradition", suggests, this pleasant upstairs emporium has a wide selection of traditional arts and crafts, especially ceramics and woodcarving, all at reasonable prices and with little of the hard sell often encountered in the nearby flea market.

▲ ANNITA PATRIKIADHOU

Leather Shop

Pandhróssou 77. A large selection of bags and purses in traditional Greek leather, and one of the remaining places where you're expected to haggle over the price.

Melissinos Art

Ayías Théklas 2, just off Ermoú ⓦwww.melissinos-art.com. The son of the Poet Sandalmaker (see above) has larger premises than his sister, packed with his own paintings and costumes, and evidence of his work as an artist, playwright and composer. Fun, but you can't help feeling these interest him more than the sandals he's supposed to be selling.

Shop

Ermoú 112a. Largest of a number of fashionable postmodern stores at the Psyrrí end of Ermoú,

Shop deals in Custo, Energie and Miss Sixty among other fashion labels, as well as gifts, books, toys and music.

Studio Kostas Sokaras

Adhrianoú 25. Overlooking the Stoa of Attalos, this place is packed with a wonderful jumble of antiques and curiosities, including old shadow puppets, brass doorknobs, musical instruments, pistols and more.

Theotokis

Normánou 7. One of a number of quirky antique/junk shops in this narrow street in the Flea Market. Prints, posters, postcards, old radios, typewriters, military uniforms: if you are looking for something specific it's amazing what they can find among their stock.

Vitallis

Pandhróssou 75. Antiquities, icons, old coins, glasswork and jewellery, as well as pieces of folk art. All in an environment that makes you feel as if you are discovering them for the first time.

Yiannis Samouelian

Iféstou 36. Long-established musical-instrument shop in the heart of the Monastiráki Flea Market, selling handmade guitars, lyra and the like.

Cafés

Hamam

Platía Ayíon Anaryíron. It seems there's a café on every corner in Psyrrí, but this is one of the best. The building was once a *hamam*, and this provides the theme – *nargileh*s (hubble-bubble pipes) and floor cushions. Coffeehouse by day

and a chilled bar by night, with tables out on the square and a summer roof terrace to escape the crowds.

Café Kornarou

Kornárou 4. A good place to interrupt your shopping trip for coffee and a sandwich, just off the bustle of the main Ermoú shopping strip. Similar cafés can be found in many of the side-streets north of Ermoú.

Café Minoas

Platía Mitropóleos, cnr Venizélou. Peaceful café on this pedestrianized square serving sandwiches, salads and ice cream.

Oréa Ellás

Mitropóleos 59 or Pandhróssou 36. 9am–6pm daily. Tucked away on the upper floor of the Kendro Ellinikis Paradosis store, this consciously old-fashioned *kafenío* offers a welcome escape from the crowded Flea Market. There's also a great view of the rooftops of Pláka on the slope towards the Acropolis.

Pagoto Manía

Aisópou 21, cnr Táki. Dozens of flavours of superb ice cream – an 8-year-old's heaven – as well as cakes, coffee and tea.

Restaurants

Café Abysinia

Kynnétou 7, Platía Avyssinías ☎ 210 32 17 047, ⊛ www.avissinia.gr. Tues–Fri 10.30am–1am, Sat & Sun 10.30am–7pm. With dining on two floors and a delicious, modern take on traditional Greek cooking (*moussaká* with spinach, for example, or

▲ BAÏRAKTARIS TAVERMA, MONASTIRAKÍ

mussel *pilaf*), *Café Abysinia* is always busy, popular with a local alternative crowd. More expensive than many, but good value for what you get, and live music most weekday evenings and weekend lunchtimes.

Baïraktaris

Mitropóleos 88, cnr Platía Monastirakíou ☎ 210 32 13 036. Over a century old, this lively restaurant occupies two buildings, the walls lined with wine barrels and photos of celebrities. Some tables are on the bustling pedestrian street but for a cosier atmosphere eat inside with the local regulars, where there's often impromptu, live traditional music. The straightforward, inexpensive menu includes *souvláki*, *yíros* and oven dishes such as *tsoutsoukákia* (meatballs in tomato sauce).

Brachera

Platía Avyssinías 3 ☎ 210 32 17 202. Eves (from 9pm) & Sun lunch only, closed Mon. Upmarket, modern Greek and Mediterranean café/bar/restaurant in a restored mansion overlooking the Flea Market. In summer, the roof garden offers views of the Acropolis.

Dhioskouri

Adhrianoú 37 ☎ 210 32 53 333. A very popular *café-mezedhopolío* with tables spreading across both sides of the pedestrianized street, some overlooking the metro lines. *Pikilía* – mixed *meze* plates – are good value at €10–15.

Elihrison

Ayíon Anaryíron 6 ☎ 5210 32 15 220. Eves only. Huge new place at the heart of Psyrrí in a tastefully restored old building with tables on several levels including a roof garden and huge internal courtyard. Pricier than most, but classier too.

Gotzila

Riga Palamídhou 5 ☎ 210 32 21 086. Eves only. Sushi bar in this über-trendy little street off Platía Ayíon Anaryíron. Mostly a late-night joint, and not badly priced.

To Kouti

Adhrianoú 23 ☎ 210 32 13 229. Innovative Greek dishes as well as pasta and salads at this enjoyable, popular and slightly alternative restaurant. The menus are scrawled by hand in old children's books; the prices are slightly higher than average.

▲ CAFÉ ABYSINIA

Mandhra

Ayíon Anaryíron 8, cnr Táki ☎210 32 13 765. Popular choice right by the main square in Psyrrí, with live music most evenings and standard taverna fare at prices that reflect the location.

Nikitas

Ayíon Anaryíron 19 ☎210 32 13 765. Lunchtime (approx 11am–6pm) only. A survivor from the days before Psyrrí was fashionable, and by far the least expensive option here, with excellent home-cooked taverna food and daily specials, plus great chips.

Palea Skala

Lepeniótou 25, cnr Leokoríou ☎210 32 52 591. Tues–Sun eves, till late. Reasonably-priced ouzerí with seating inside an old house and on a terrace in summer. Excellent *mezédhes* and wine to accompany the acoustic house band; generally packed and lots of fun.

Taverna Platía Iróon

Platía Iróon 1 ☎210 32 11 915. With tables set out on the less crowded square in Psyrrí, this is a great place for people-watching; inside, there's often live music in the evening. The food includes excellent *fáva* (hummus-like bean purée) and taverna standards, good value for the location.

Taverna tou Psyrri

Eskhýlou 12 ☎210 32 14 923. Some of the lowest prices and tastiest food in Psyrrí, so unsurprisingly popular. The menu is an unusual take on Greek classics, and is written in deliberately obscure Greek, so it may be easier to choose from the kitchen. Garden courtyard seating at the back is accessed via an alleyway alongside the next-door restaurant.

Thanasis

Mitropóleos 69. Reckoned to serve the best *souvláki* and *yíros* in this part of Athens, where there's plenty of competition. Inexpensive, and always packed with locals at lunchtime: there's no booking, so you'll have to fight for a table. Watch out for the side dish of peppers, which are unusually fiery.

Zidhoron

Táki 10, cnr Ayíon Anaryíron ☎210 32 15 368. Closed Aug. A typical Psyrrí upscale *mezhedopolío*, painted bright yellow and in a great location offering a vantage point over the goings-on of the area. It serves tasty Middle-Eastern foods like *pastourmás*, *haloúmi* and hummus, as well as Greek favourites such as baked feta, grilled peppers and baked aubergine.

Bars

Alekos Island

Sarrí 41, Psyrrí ☏ 693 89 59 549.
Alekos is one of Athens' more colourful bartenders, and his long-established, easy-going gay bar has recently moved down from Kolonáki to this livelier location. Low-key atmosphere and rocky/poppy music. Open nightly, year-round.

Arodou

Miaoúli, cnr Protoyénous. Miaoúli is packed with bars and crowded with people every evening. *Arodou* is right at the heart – a big place with plenty of space both outside and in. Not fancy at all, but a good place to meet up before moving on and decent food available if you want it.

Astron

Táki 3 ☏ 697 74 69 356. Eves only.
One of Psyrrí's busiest bars – partly perhaps because it's so small – which gets really packed when the guest DJs crank it up later on.

Mooi

Miaoúli 6, cnr Thémidos ☏ 210 32 12 624. Closed Sun. Thanks to a location right by an exit from Monastiráki metro station on the way up to Psyrrí, this cool, modern, moodily lit bar is a popular meeting place. Food is served during the day.

Soul

Evripídhou 65 ☏ 210 33 10 907.
Laid-back, popular, upstairs cocktail bar (also serving Thai-influenced food) with alternative sounds.

Clubs

Blaze-T

Aristophánous 30 ☏ 210 32 34 823.
11pm–4am. Freestyle disco, long-established by Psyrrí standards, with sounds ranging from hip-hop to techno.

Candy Bar/Meine Danza

Aristophánous 11 ☏ 210 33 17 105. Hang out at *Candy Bar*, downstairs, earlier in the evening, then move up to *Danza* later, where guest DJs might be playing anything from house to retro rock.

Cubanita

Karaïskáki 28 ☏ 210 33 14 605.
Enjoyable Cuban-themed bar/restaurant/club, with plenty of rum-based drinks, Cuban food and Latin music, occasionally live. Party atmosphere till the early hours.

Moresko

Aristophánous 17 ☏ 210 32 41 249.
Moorish theme complete with belly dancers most nights in this ultra-cool, elegant club.

Temple of the King

Agathárkhou 5 ☏ 210 33 18 311. One of a couple of chilled music clubs in this alley in the heart of Psyrrí; all kinds of sounds but primarily rock.

Thissío, Gázi and Áno Petrálona

Some of the most interesting up-and-coming areas of Athens – Thissío, Gázi and neighbouring Roúf – lie to the west of the centre, where a new extension to Metro line 3, beyond Monastiráki, can only accelerate the pace of change. Nightlife and restaurants are the chief attractions here, but there's also a cluster of new museums and galleries, above all the Tekhnópolis centre and two annexes of the Benáki Museum, devoted to Islamic and modern art respectively.

Here too is Kerameikos, site of the cemetery of ancient Athens and a substantial section of its walls. South of Thissío, things are rather more traditional. Pedestrianized Apóstolou Pávlou leads around the edge of the Agora and Acropolis sites, under the flanks of the hills of the Pnyx and Filopáppou, and offers a pleasant, green escape from the city as well as fine views.

On the west side of the hills, the residential zone of Áno Petrálona is a real delight, entirely untouristy, with some

excellent tavernas (see p.92) and a great open-air cinema, though absolutely nothing in the way of sights. Between them, these places offer some excellent and authentic eating and drinking options – a welcome antidote to Pláka's tourist traps. You'll find everything from the lively, youth-oriented bars, clubs and restaurants of Gázi to positively sleepy, old-fashioned tavernas in Áno Petrálona. Thissío, easily accessible by metro, has a good mix, with some of the best evening and night-time views of the Acropolis from cafés

▼ DHIONYSÍOU AREOPAYÍTOU

▲ VIEW FROM FILOPÁPPOU HILL

around the traffic-free junction of Apóstolou Pávlou and Iraklidhón.

Filopáppou Hill

From around the junction of Apóstolou Pávlou and Dhionysíou Areopayítou, below the Acropolis entrance, a network of paths leads up Filopáppou Hill, known in antiquity as the "Hill of the Muses". Its pine- and cypress-clad slopes provide fabulous views of the Acropolis and the city beyond, especially at sunset (although night-time muggings have occurred here, so take care).

This strategic height has played an important, if generally sorry, role in the city's history. In 1687 it was from here that the shell that destroyed the roof of the Parthenon was lobbed; more recently, the colonels placed tanks on the slopes during their coup of 1967. The hill's summit is capped by a grandiose monument to a Roman senator and consul, Filopappus, who is depicted driving his chariot on its frieze. To the west is the Dora Stratou Theatre (see p.183). On the way up the hill, the main path follows a line of truncated ancient walls, past the attractive sixteenth-century church of **Áyios Dhimítrios**, inside which are some original Byzantine frescoes. Further down, in the rock-face near the base of the hill, you can make out a kind of cave dwelling, known (more from imagination than evidence) as the prison of Socrates.

The Pnyx and Hill of the Nymphs

In Classical times the Hill of the Pnyx was the meeting place of the democratic assembly, which gathered more than forty times a year. All except the most serious political issues were aired here, where a convenient semicircular terrace makes a natural spot from which to address the crowd. All male citizens could vote and, at least in theory, all could voice their opinions, though the assembly was harsh on inarticulate or foolish speakers. There are some impressive remains of the original walls, which formed the theatre-like court, and of *stoas* where the assembly would have taken refreshment. This atmospheric setting provides commanding Acropolis views, while benches on the west side allow you to contemplate the vista across Pireás and out to sea. On

PLACES

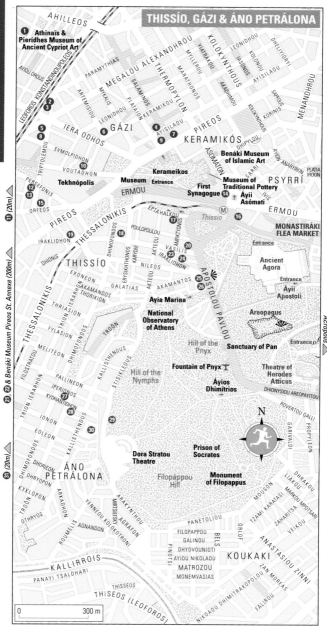

THISSÍO, GÁZI & ÁNO PETRÁLONA

RESTAURANTS					
T'Askimopapo	30	Mamacas	12	Stavlos	24
Chez Lucien	27	Meson el Mirador	4	To Steki tou Ilia	17
Dirty Str-eat	8	Pil Poul	20	Thalatta	19
Epistrofi stin Ithaki	18	Prosopa	3	Varoulko	7
Ikonomou	28	Santorinios	31	Votanikos Steak House	1
To Koutouki	29	Skoufias	21	Zei	6

BARS		CAFÉS		CLUBS		LIVE MUSIC	
45°	10	aPLAKAfé	16	Club 22	11	Gazi	22
Bios	9	Athinaion Politeia	25	Code	15		
Blue Train	2	Kirki	26	Luv	14		
Space by Avli	23			Sodade	5		
Tapas Bar	13						

PLACES Thissío, Gázi and Áno Petrálona

the northern slope, above Thissío, stands the impressive, Neoclassical bulk of the **National Observatory of Athens** (Ⓦ www.noa.gr; open first Fri of every month).

Over to the west a third hill rises – the **Hill of the Nymphs**. Nymphs were associated with the dusty whirlwinds to which this hill is particularly prone and it is said to be the location of the fairy sequences in Shakespeare's *Midsummer Night's Dream*. Slightly lower and quieter than its better-known neighbours, this is a peaceful place with good views across to the western suburbs of Athens and beyond, as well as pleasant shaded walks.

Apóstolou Pávlou

Beneath the hills you can follow pedestrianized Apóstolou Pávlou right around the edge of the Ancient Agora and Acropolis sites from Metro Thissío to the Acropolis entrance. It's a rewarding walk especially in the early evening, when the setting sun illuminates this side of the rock and the cafés of Thissío start to fill with an anticipatory buzz. As you follow the street round there are a number of small excavations at the base of the hills. Perhaps the most interesting is the Sanctuary of

Pan, on the lower slopes of the Pnyx just beyond the Thission open-air cinema. The cult of Pan was associated with caves, and in this fenced-off site you can see the opening to an underground chamber cut into the rock. Inside were found reliefs of Pan, a naked nymph, and a dog. There's also a mosaic floor and, nearby, remains of an ancient road and two rock-cut, Classical-era houses. Just above the sanctuary is the so-called Fountain of Pnyx. In the sixth century BC a water system was engineered, with subterranean pipes bringing water from springs to cisterns that supplied the city. This is believed to be one of those: behind a locked entrance is a chamber with a Roman mosaic floor where the water was collected. You can also see traces of the concrete used to seal the chamber during World War II, when valuable antiquities were stored inside.

Kerameikos

Entrance on Ermoú. Daily: April–Sept 8am–7.30pm; Oct–March 8.30am–3pm; museum opens 11am Mon. €2 or joint Acropolis ticket. The Kerameikos (or Keramikós) site, encompassing the principal cemetery of ancient Athens and a hefty section of the ancient wall, provides a fascinating and quiet retreat. Little visited, it has something of an oasis feel, with the lush Iridhanós channel, speckled with water lilies, flowing across the site from east to west.

To the right of the entrance is the stream and the double line of the city wall. Two roads pierced the defences here, and the gates that marked their entrance to the city have been excavated: the great Dipylon Gate was the busiest in the ancient city, where the road from Pireás, Eleusis and the north arrived; the Sacred Gate was a ceremonial entrance where the Ierá Odhós or Sacred Way entered the city – it was used for the Eleusinian and Panathenaic processions (see p.148 & p.54).

Branching off to the left from the Sacred Way, the Street of the Tombs, which is actually the old road to Pireás, heads through the cemetery. Numerous commemorative monuments have been excavated alongside the road, and their original stones reinstated or replaced by replicas. The flat vertical stelae were the main funerary monuments of the Classical world; the sarcophagi that you see are later, from Hellenistic or Roman times. The large tomb with the massive semicircular base to the left of the path is the Memorial of Dexileos, the 20-year-old son of Lysanias of Thorikos, who was killed in action at Corinth in 394 BC. The adjacent plot contains the Monument of Dionysios of Kollytos, in the shape of a pillar stele supporting a bull carved from Pentelic marble.

The new site museum is a lovely, cool, marble-floored space displaying finds from the site and related material, above all stelae and grave markers. There are also many poignant funerary offerings – toys from child burials, gold jewellery and beautiful small objects of all sorts. The ceramics are particularly fine, including lovely dishes with horses on their lids (*pyxides*) from the early eighth century BC and some stunning fifth-century-BC black-and-red figure pottery.

Benáki Museum of Islamic Art

Áyion Asomáton 22, cnr Dhípylou @ www.benaki.gr. Tues & Thurs–Sun 9am–3pm, Wed 9am–9pm. €5. Antonis Benakis, founder of the Benáki Museum (p.123), spent much of his life in Egypt and this new museum, in a converted Neoclassical mansion, was created to house the collection he amassed there. It follows a chronological course up through the building, from the seventh century on the first floor to the nineteenth on the fourth. Throughout there are beautiful, intricately decorated objects in almost every type of art: ceramics (especially tiles), metalwork and wood above all, but also textiles, jewellery, glass, scientific instruments, armour and more. The highlights, perhaps, are on the third floor, from the sixteenth- and seventeenth-century Golden Age of the Ottoman Empire under Sulëyman the Magnificent. Here is a reconstructed room from a Cairo mansion, complete with inlaid marble floor, sunken fountains, elaborate wooden window-screens, as well as silk wall-hangings (not from the mansion), shot with silver and gold thread. There's a top-floor café overlooking the Kerameikos site with industrial Gázi beyond, as

▲ TEKHNÓPOLIS

well as views of the Acropolis and Filopáppou, while in the basement can be seen a substantial chunk of the ancient city wall, almost 6m high, that was preserved during the building's restoration.

Museum of Traditional Pottery

Melidhóni 4. Mon–Fri 9am–3pm, Sat 10am–2pm. €6. A tiny place (and therefore pricey for what you get), the Museum of Traditional Pottery has a series of small rooms with exhibits on traditional pottery-making methods, complete with regular hands-on demonstrations. A couple of further galleries have temporary exhibits, usually on a particular style or era of pottery. Completing the ensemble is a small café and a shop selling quality ceramics.

Tekhnópolis

Pireós 100 ☎ 210 34 67 322. Daily 10am–10pm. The former gasworks from which the Gázi district takes its name has been converted into a stunning series of spaces for concerts and changing exhibitions, mostly of contemporary art and photography. Two round

gas-holders have become circular glass offices – one for Athens 98.4FM, the other for Tekhnópolis administration – while in the various pumping stations and boiler rooms surrounding them, galleries and exhibition halls of varying sizes, as well as a café, have been created, many with parts of the original machinery preserved. The only permanent display here is a small Maria Callas Museum (Mon–Fri 10am–5pm; free), whose collection of personal letters and photos, plus a pair of gloves and a fur coat, is really for fans only. All sorts of temporary exhibitions and concerts take place, though, so it's well worth taking a look – or check local listings magazines for details.

Benáki Museum Pireós Street Annexe

Pireós 138, cnr Andhrónikou ⓦwww .benaki.gr. Wed, Thurs, Sun 10am–6pm, Fri & Sat 10am–10pm. Exhibition prices vary. Metro Petrálona, or many buses along Pireós including 049, 914 and trolley 021. Some six long blocks southwest of Tekhnópolis, the new Benáki cultural centre is symptomatic of the development that is transforming a formerly industrial part of the city centre. There's no permanent collection here, but the prestige of the Benáki Museum can attract exceptional temporary shows so it's always worth checking out what's on. The vast industrial space, now clad in pink marble, has been cleverly converted to galleries on various levels around an internal courtyard: be sure to explore as it's not always obvious what's on where. There's an airy, upmarket indoor restaurant/café, too, serving sandwiches and salads as well as more substantial dishes.

Athinaïs

Kastoriás 34–36 ☎ 210 34 80 000, ⓦ www.athinais.com.gr. A magnificent restoration of an early twentieth-century silk factory, the Athinaïs complex contains a theatre, music space, movie screen, two restaurants, a bar and café, exhibition halls, a museum and, the real purpose of the place, a sizeable conference centre. The **Pierídhes Museum of Ancient Cypriot Art** (daily 9.30am–7pm; €3) is beautifully presented in four small galleries, with some top-class exhibits including ceramics and very early glassware – although it might seem strange to be admiring these Cypriot objects in Athens. The museum shop is full of lavish (and lavishly priced) arty gifts, while upstairs are art galleries with temporary exhibitions. Details of what's on can be found on the website or in the local press.

Cafés

aPLAKAfé

Adhrianoú 1. Right by Platía Thissíou, this large, busy café is a popular place to meet up. Breakfasts, light snacks, sandwiches and meals served as well as the ubiquitous coffees and frappés, and with tables outside as well as in a courtyard that's covered in winter. By night, there's music and more of a bar atmosphere.

Athinalon Politeia

Akamántos 1, cnr Apóstolou Pávlou. An enviable position in an old mansion, with great views from the terrace towards the Acropolis, makes this an excellent place to relax over a frappé. Light meals also served.

Kirki

Apostólou Pávlou 31. Another café with a fabulous Acropolis view from its outdoor tables, serving good *mezédhes* as well as drinks and ice creams. Popular with the clientele of the late-night gay club (*Lizard*) upstairs.

Restaurants

T'Askimopapo

Iónon 61 ☎ 210 34 63 282. Closed Sun & mid-May to mid-Sept. A wonderful winter-only taverna with *mezédhes* and unusual main dishes. Occasional live music, and rooftop dining for balmy days.

Chez Lucien

Tróon 32 ☎ 210 34 64 236. Tues–Sat 8.30pm–1am. Excellent French bistro with a short menu of authentic, well-prepared dishes at reasonable prices; you may have to share a table. No booking and very popular, so turn up early or very late.

Dirty Str-eat

Triptolémou 12 ☎ 210 34 74 763. Eves only, closed Sun. Popular

bar-restaurant with a garden courtyard at the back – originally specialized in fish, which is still a good choice, but now has a broader, simpler menu.

Epistrofi stin Ithaki

Iraklidhón 56 ☎210 34 72 964. Mon–Sat 9am–9pm, Sun 1–9pm. Tiny, unpretentious place attached to an equally small organic food and craft shop, serving inexpensive organic *meze*s, including plenty of vegetarian choices.

Ikonomou

Tróon 41, cnr Kydhantidhon ☎210 34 67 555. Closed Sun. Wonderful traditional taverna with home-cooked food served to packed pavement tables in summer. No menu, just a dozen or so inexpensive daily specials: check out what others are eating as the waiters may not know the names of some of the dishes in English.

To Koutouki

Lakíou 9 (reached from Filopáppou hill, or by a tunnel under the main road) ☎210 34 53 655. Closed Sun. Inexpensive traditional taverna with good *fáva* and grilled meat. Pleasantly rural atmosphere despite the proximity of the flyover, with no houses nearby and roof seating overlooking Filopáppou Hill.

Mamacas

Persefónis 41 ☎210 34 64 984. One of the restaurants that made Gázi fashionable, and still a favourite with the young, stylish and well-heeled. The white decor spreads through a house and across several terraces. Service can be slow, but the food – traditional Greek, *mezédhes*-style, with a modern twist – is reliably good. It's fairly pricey and, like everywhere

▲ CHEZ LUCIEN

here, doesn't get lively till late – some time after midnight, the DJs take over. Booking advised.

Meson el Mirador

Ayisiláou 88, cnr Salamínos ☎210 34 20 007. Closed Sun. Authentic Mexican restaurant in an elegant restored mansion in Keramikós. Gets enjoyably rowdy later on.

Pil Poul

Apostólou Pávlou 51, cnr Poulopoúlou ☎210 34 23 665. Closed Mon. Fancy and expensive modern French/Mediterranean restaurant. The food is occasionally over-elaborate, but the roof terrace in this 1920s mansion offers immaculate Acropolis views in an incomparably romantic setting. There's a chilled-out bar/club (also *Pil Poul*) downstairs in the same building. Booking essential.

Prosopa

Konstantinoupóleos 84 ☎210 34 13 433. Very popular, somewhat upmarket restaurant serving excellent modern Mediterranean food – Greek with Italian and French influences. Tables are set out alongside the railway lines as

▲ MAMACAS

well as indoors, in an area of Gázi with numerous gay clubs.

Santorinios

Dhorién 8 ☎ 210 34 51 629.
Unpretentious "wine-taverna" whose main decoration is provided by vast barrels of Santorini wine. Swill it down with good *mezédhes* in the whitewashed courtyard.

Skoufias

Vasilíou Megálou 50 ☎ 210 34 12 252. Eves only, closed Mon. Fine taverna with Cretan and other unusual regional dishes, off the beaten track in Roúf (just beyond Gázi) but well worth seeking out – the honey-roast pork is the house speciality.

Stavlos

Iraklidhón 10 ☎ 210 34 67 206, ⓦ www.stavlos.gr. Mon–Thurs eves only, Fri–Sun from midday. Originally used as royal stables during the nineteenth century, *Stavlos* is now one of the more popular meeting points in the area with numerous seating areas including a large internal courtyard. Italian-influenced restaurant, as well as a bar, gallery and club.

To Steki tou Ilia

Eptahálkou 5 ☎ 210 34 58 052. Closed Sun. Simple, inexpensive place on a pedestrianized street above the metro tracks that's so popular the owners have opened a second branch 200m further down (at Thessaloníkis 7). Renowned for some of the finest lamb chops in the city. Tables out in the street in summer.

Thalatta

Vítonos 5 ☎ 210 34 64 204. Eves only, closed Sun. A lovely, upmarket seafood restaurant (*Thalatta* means "sea" in Ancient Greek), in a thoroughly unprepossessing location. Marine decor and an internal courtyard in summer.

Varoulko

Pireós 80 ☎ 210 52 28 400 ⓦ www .varoulko.gr. Eves only, closed Sun. Chef Lefteris Lazarou earned a Michelin star for his restaurant in Piraeus: now downtown, the prices reflect that (€80 or more a head). When they come off, though, the elaborate and innovative seafood dishes are worth it: the cool, modern setting includes a summer roof terrace with Acropolis views. Booking essential.

Votanikos Steak House

Kastoriás 34–36 ☎ 210 34 80 000. Steaks, obviously, but also a broad menu of alternatives in this big, modern, brasserie-style place in the Athinaïs complex.

Zei

Artemisíou 4, cnr Keramikoú ☎ 210 34 60 076. Eves & Sun lunch only; closed Mon & Tues. Charming old house serving imaginative Anatolian and Greek *mezédhes* in an enclosed courtyard. Best Thurs–Sat when it's busy and there's live rebétika and laïká music.

Bars

45°

Iákhou 18, cnr Voutadhon ☏ 210 34 72 729. A big, lively, rock-music-based bar-club with a rooftop terrace in summer.

Bios

Pireós 84, Gázi ☏ 210 34 25 335. Boho art-space/café/bar with frequent happenings of performance art or experimental theatre. There's something going on here most evenings, and a basement dance-space with late-night avant-garde sounds.

Blue Train

Konstantinoupóleos 84 ☏ 210 34 60 677. With a courtyard in summer, and open from early evening, this is a popular gay meeting-place before going on to the clubs. Upstairs, *Kazarma* (same phone, ⓦ www.ka3arma .gr) is one of the better clubs you could go on to, with dance music, laser shows and giant screens.

Space by Avli

Iraklidhón 14. In the heart of the Thissío bar area, this daytime café/bar on three floors evolves at night into a funky club with jazz and soul sounds.

Tapas Bar

Triptolémou 44 ☏ 210 34 71 844. Eves only, closed Sun. Despite the name you won't find many people eating the *tapas* here, but it's busy and buzzy till the early hours –handy for the Gázi clubs – with good cocktails and a pleasant outdoor space.

Clubs

Club 22

Dhekeléon 26 ☏ 210 34 52 220, ⓦ www.club22.gr. Daily midnight–4.30am. Huge club with wild theme-nights and visiting DJs: party atmosphere and anything from hip-hop to old-school 80s nights.

Code

Triptolémou 35 ☏ 210 34 58 118. Daily midnight–4.30am. Small gay club that packs in the crowds with Greek music.

Luv

Asomáton 1, Platía Thissíou ☏ 210 32 24 553. Big, mainstream dance-club with DJ guest nights and a young crowd.

Sodade

Triptolémou 10 ☏ 210 34 68 657, ⓦ www.sodade.gr. Nightly from 11pm. Stylish gay and lesbian crowd and great music – one room plays Greek and mainstream, the other quality dance music.

Live music

Gazi

Ierofándos 9 at Pireós, Roúf ☏ 210 34 74 477. Big *bouzoúkia* (glitzy modern Greek music) club in an up-and-coming industrial area just down from Gázi – as a result attracts a younger crowd than some.

Sýndagma and around

All roads lead to Sýndagma – you'll almost inevitably find yourself here sooner or later for the metro and bus connections. Platía Syndágmatos, Constitution Square, to give it its full name, lies roughly midway between the Acropolis and Lykavitós Hill. With the Greek Parliament building (the Voulí) on its uphill side, and banks, offices and embassies clustered around, it's the political and geographic heart of Athens.

The square's name derives from the fact that Greece's first constitution was proclaimed (reluctantly under popular pressure) by King Otto from the palace balcony in 1843. It's still the principal venue for mass demonstrations, and in the run-up to elections the major political parties stage their final campaign rallies here.

Vital hub as it is, however, the traffic and the crush ensure it's not an attractive place to hang around. Escape comes in the form of the National Gardens, a welcome area of greenery stretching out south from the parliament building and offering a traffic-free route down

past the Záppio to Hadrian's Arch and the Temple of Olympian Zeus, or across to the Panathenaic Stadium (p.130). In other directions Odhós Ermoú, prime shopping territory, heads west towards Monastiráki, with Pláka and the Acropolis to the southwest; Stadhíou and Panepistimíou head northwest towards Omonía; while to the north and east lie Kolonáki and the embassy quarter.

Hotel Grande Bretagne

Vasiléos Yeoryíou 1 ☎ 210 33 30 000, ⓦ www.grandebretagne.gr. With the exception of the Voulí, the vast *Hotel Grande Bretagne* – Athens' grandest – is just about the only

▼ PARLIAMENT BUILDING

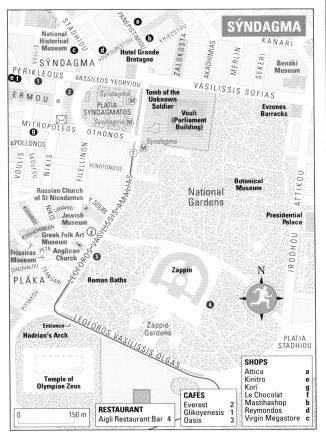

building on Sýndagma to have
survived postwar development.
Past the impressive facade
and uniformed doormen,
the interior is magnificently
opulent, as befits a grand hotel
established in the late nineteenth
century. It's worth taking a look
inside, or having a drink at one
of the bars: renovation in 2003
included a new rooftop pool,
bar and restaurant with great
views across the city.

The hotel has long been at
the centre of Greek political
intrigue: in one notorious
episode, Winston Churchill
narrowly avoided being blown
up here on Christmas Day
1944, when saboteurs from the
Communist-led ELAS resistance
movement placed an enormous
explosive charge in the drains.
According to whom you
believe, the bomb was either
discovered in time by a kitchen
employee, or removed by ELAS
themselves when they realized
that Churchill was one of their
potential victims.

The Voulí

Platía Syndágmatos. Not open to the public. The Greek National Parliament, the Voulí, presides over Platía Syndágmatos from its uphill (east) side. A vast, ochre-and-white Neoclassical structure, it was built as the royal palace for Greece's first monarch, the Bavarian King Otto, who moved in in 1842. In front of it, goose-stepping *evzónes* in tasselled caps, kilt and woolly leggings – a prettified version of traditional mountain costume – change their guard at intervals in front of the Tomb of the Unknown Soldier. On Sundays, just before 11am, a full band and the entire corps parade from the tomb to their barracks at the back of the National Gardens to the rhythm of innumerable camera shutters.

The National Gardens

Entrances on Amalías, Vasilíssis Sofías, and Iródhou Attikoú. Daily sunrise–sunset. Free. The most refreshing acres in the city are the National Gardens – not so much a flower garden as a luxuriant tangle of trees, whose shade and duck ponds provide palpable relief from the heat in summer. The gardens were originally the private palace gardens, a pet project of Queen Amalia in the 1840s; supposedly the main duty of the tiny Greek navy in its early days was to fetch rare plants, often the gifts of other royal houses, from remote corners of the globe. Despite a major pre-Olympics clear-out, there's still something of an air of benign neglect here, with rampant undergrowth and signs that seem to take you round in circles.

It's a great place for a picnic, though, or just a shady respite from the city streets. There are benches everywhere, ducks being fed in the ponds, and other attractions including a small zoo, a children's playground (on the Záppio side) and a botanical museum. The tiny zoo (signed *Irattikou*) has ostriches and some exotic fowl, but most of the cages these days are occupied by chickens, rabbits and domestic cats. The **Botanical Museum** occupies an elegant little pavilion nearby; closed for refurbishment at the time of writing.

On the far side of the gardens is the **Presidential Palace**,

▼ THE NATIONAL GARDENS

▲ ZÁPPIO

the royal residence until Constantine's exile in 1967, where more *evzónes* stand on sentry duty.

The Záppio

Open 24hr. On the southern side of the National Gardens are the graceful, crescent-shaped grounds of the Záppio. Popular with evening and weekend strollers, they're more open, and more formally laid out. The Záppio itself, an imposing Neoclassical edifice originally built as an exhibition hall, is not open to the public. Although it has no permanent function, the building has taken on prestigious roles such as the headquarters for both the Greek presidency of the European Union and of the 2004 Olympic bid.

Hadrian's Arch

Leofóros Amalías. Hadrian's Arch stands in splendid isolation on what feels like one of the busiest corners in Athens, where Odhós Syngroú arrives in the centre of town. With the traffic roaring by, this is not somewhere you are tempted to linger – but it's definitely worth a look on your way to the Temple of Olympian Zeus.

The arch, eighteen metres high, was erected by the emperor to mark the edge of the Classical city and the beginning of his own. On the west side its frieze is inscribed "This is Athens, the ancient city of Theseus", and on the other "This is the City of Hadrian and not of Theseus". With so little that's ancient remaining around it, this doesn't make immediate sense, but you can look up, westwards, to the Acropolis and in the other direction see the columns of the great temple completed by Hadrian. Many more Roman remains are thought to lie under the Záppio area, and over towards the old Olympic Stadium. Concrete evidence of this lies in a large Roman Baths complex that was discovered alongside the Záppio gardens during excavations for the Metro. Dating originally from the late third century AD and substantially expanded over succeeding centuries, the baths are now visible under a metal and perspex cover alongside the busy avenue. Complete rooms have been well preserved and are now exposed to the gaze.

▲ HADRIAN'S ARCH

The Temple of Olympian Zeus

Entrance on Vasilíssis Ólgas. Daily: April–Sept 8am–7.30pm; Oct–March 8.30am–3pm. €2, or joint Acropolis ticket. The colossal pillars of the Temple of Olympian Zeus – also known as the Olympieion – stand in the middle of a huge, dusty clearing with excellent views of the Acropolis and constant traffic noise. One of the largest temples in the ancient world – and according to Livy "the only temple on earth to do justice to the god" – it was dedicated by Hadrian in 131 AD, almost 700 years after the tyrant Peisistratos had begun work on it. Hadrian marked the occasion by contributing an enormous statue of Zeus and an equally monumental one of himself, although both have since been lost. Just fifteen of the temple's original 104 marble pillars remain erect, though the massive column drums of another, which fell in 1852, litter the ground, giving a startling idea of the project's size. To the north of the temple enclosure, by the site entrance, are various excavated remains including an impressive Roman bath complex and a gateway from the wall of the Classical city. The south side of the enclosure overlooks a further area of excavation (not open to the public) where both Roman and much earlier buildings have been revealed.

Shops

Attica

Panepistimíou 9. Athens' only fashion department store, with the finest window displays in the city. Convenient if you want to do everything under one roof, especially in the summer when it's hot, though the designer labels include nothing you wouldn't find at home.

Kinitro

Karayeóryi Servías 11. Cheap and cheerful jewellery shop with a modern feel, or you can design your own on the spot.

Kori

Mitropóleos 13 and Voúlis. Very high-standard craftwork in silver, gold and ceramic with prices to match. Beautiful original designs with some traditional influences.

Le Chocolat

Karayeóryi Servías 3. If chocolate is your weakness, you'll find Belgian, French and Greek in this small emporium.

Mastihashop

Panepistimíou, cnr Kriezótou ⓦwww .mastihashop.com. Using extracts from the famous mastic gum from the island of Chios, a variety of products – from cosmetics to edible gourmet delicacies – are available in designer-quality packaging, all with the distinctive and yet delicate aroma of therapeutic mastic.

▲ TEMPLE OF OLYMPIAN ZEUS

Reymondos

Voukourestíou 18. Small bookshop, good for foreign periodicals in particular.

Virgin Megastore

Stadhíou 7–9. Not terribly inspired, but does exactly what you'd expect – a wide variety of regulation hits and Greek pop.

Cafés

Everest

Ermoú 2, Platía Sindágmatos. Daily 24 hr. With an *Easy Internet Café* upstairs, this branch of the sandwich chain is always busy. While you can eat in, you may prefer to collect a picnic to take to the National Gardens.

Oasis

West side of National Gardens, opposite cnr of Amalías and Filellínon. This café just off the main avenue is an unexpected haven, offering ice cream, ouzo and *mezédhes* in the shade.

Glikoyenesis

Karayeóryi Servías 9, cnr Voúlis. Handy for Sýndagma and the local shops, the so-called *Yellow Café* serves excellent coffee, sandwiches and salads by day and morphs into a quiet cocktail bar at night.

Restaurants

Aigli Restaurant Bar

Záppio gardens on the east side of the Záppio ☎210 33 69 300, ⊛www.aeglizappiou.gr. Pricey, smart restaurant with a fabulous setting, allegedly the haunt of the rich and famous, and certainly popular with politicians and diplomats. "Modern Mediterranean" food, which here means Greek with French and Italian influences. A bar, open-air cinema and nightclub are part of the same complex.

Platía Omonías and the bazaar

While Pláka and Sýndagma are resolutely geared to tourists and the Athenian well-heeled, Platía Omonías (Omonía Square) and its surroundings represent a much more gritty city, revolving around everyday commerce and trade. Here the grand avenues imagined by the nineteenth-century planners have been subverted by time and the realities of Athens' status as a commercial capital.

Leaving Sýndagma on Stadhíou or Panepistimíou, there are at first grandiose mansions, some converted to museums, squares with open vistas, and chichi shopping: you don't have to go far, though, before the shops get smaller, the *stoa*s more run down, the buildings less shiny. Heading up from Monastiráki, the bazaar area around Odhós Athinás is home to a bustling series of markets and small stores spilling into the streets and offering some of urban

Athens' most compelling sights and sounds, as well as an ethnic mix that is a rare reminder of Greece's traditional role as a meeting place of East and West.

To the west of Omonía, towards the rail stations, Metaxouryío is an area undergoing something of a revival as development spills over from fashionable neighbouring Psyrrí and Gázi. As far as more conventional sights go, the area is home to a clutch of small, specialist museums and a series of elegant Neoclassical buildings strung out between Sýndagma and Omonía, a legacy of the ambitious building programme that followed Greece's independence in 1821.

The Market

The modern market or bazaar is concentrated on Athinás and Eólou streets. Here the stores, though stocked mainly with imported manufactured goods, still reflect their origins in the Oriental souk system: their unaffected decor, unsophisticated packaging and, most strikingly, their specialization. Though it's a tradition that's gradually dying, each street still has a

▼ OMONÍA SQUARE

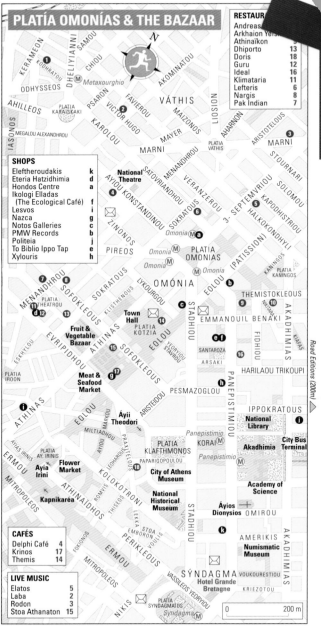

PLATÍA OMONÍAS & THE BAZAAR

RESTAUR...

Andreas	
Arkhaion Yers...	
Athinaïkon	9
Dhiporto	13
Doris	18
Guru	12
Ideal	16
Klimataria	11
Lefteris	6
Nargis	8
Pak Indian	7

SHOPS

Eleftheroudakis	k
Eteria Hatzidhimia	d
Hondos Centre	a
Ikologi Elladas (The Ecological Café)	f
Lesvos	i
Nazca	g
Notos Galleries	c
PMW Records	b
Politeia	j
To Biblio Ippo Tap	e
Xylouris	h

CAFÉS

Delphi Café	4
Krinos	17
Themis	14

LIVE MUSIC

Elatos	5
Laba	2
Rodon	3
Stoa Athanaton	15

▲ SEAFOOD MARKET

concentration of particular stores and wares. Hence the Monastiráki end of Athinás is dedicated to tools; food stores are gathered around the central market in the middle, especially along Evripídhou; there's glass to the west; paint and brasswork to the east; and clothes in Eólou and Ayíou Márkou. Around Evripídhou, a growing community from South Asia, predominantly Bengalis, gathers in large numbers around spice-rich minimarkets and cheap and cheerful curry houses. Always raucous and teeming with shoppers, *kouloúri* (bread-ring) sellers, gypsies and other vendors, the whole area is great free entertainment.

At its heart lies the **meat and seafood market**, set in a grand nineteenth-century building. Its fretted iron awnings shelter forests of carcasses and mounds of hearts, livers and ears – no place for the squeamish. In the middle section of the hall is the fish market, with all manner of bounty from the sea glistening on marble slabs.

Across Athinás from here, the **fruit and vegetable bazaar** is a riot of colours and noise, as the vendors shout their wares. In the surrounding streets grocers pile their stalls high with sacks of pulses, salt cod, barrels of olives and wheels of cheese.

Odhós Eólou: the Flower Market and Platía Kótzia

Odhós Eólou seems far less frantic than parallel Athinás, partly because it is pedestrianized. Local businesses take advantage of this, with café tables in the street, and benches to rest on. Its gentler nature perhaps reflects the goods sold here: where Athinás has power tools and raw meat, Eólou offers clothes and the Flower Market. The latter, gathered around the church of Ayía Iríni at the southern end of the street, has stalls through the week but, with the crowds, it really comes alive on a Sunday morning.

At the northern end of the street, Platía Kótzia is a far more formal enclave, and one of the city's more impressive examples of Olympic refurbishment. Surrounded by the town hall and the weighty Neoclassical buildings of the National Bank, it's a rare glimpse of elegant old Athens, spoiled only by the crumbling modern blocks above the Post Office. In the middle of the square a large section of ancient road has been uncovered and can be seen in a fenced-off site – numerous tombs and small buildings lie alongside it. This road, just outside the walls, once led to one of the main gates of ancient Athens and this too has recently been excavated, during building work for a new Stock Exchange. You can see this gate and some of the adjoining city wall underneath the new building, between Platía Kótzia and Sofokléous; nearby more sections of the ancient road and a drainage system are visible under glass pyramids in the middle of Eólou. The sight of the Acropolis from this street as you approached Athens in ancient times must have been awe-inspiring, and Eólou still has impressive views today, with the Erechtheion's slender columns and pediment peeking over the edge of the crag straight ahead.

Platía Omonías

Platía Omonías has little to offer in terms of aesthetics, but it is the heart of Athens for a good portion of the population. A continuous turmoil of people and cars, it is Athens at its earthiest and most urban. Cleaning-up and remodelling for the Olympics has removed much of the area's character – no bad thing, some would say, as that character derived from druggies, prostitutes and homeless Albanian refugees – and the new look is ugly, brutal and shadeless. Even sanitized, though, Omonía seems to retain a generally seedy atmosphere, the perimeter of the square dominated by kiosks whose chief trade seems to be in porn, clustered in front of a mishmash of fast-food outlets and discount stores. The streets surrounding the square are full of offices, high-rise hotels and functional shopping.

National Historical Museum

Stadhíou 13, Platía Kolokotróni. Tues–Sun 9am–2pm. €3. Occupying a building that housed the Greek parliament from 1874 until 1935, the National Historical Museum focuses on Greek history from the fall of Constantinople to the reign of King Otto, with particular emphasis on the Byzantine era. There's also a strong section on the War of Independence that includes Byron's sword and helmet. Unfortunately, minimal labelling leaves the visitor a little short of the historical context of the displays.

Platía Klafthomónos: the City of Athens Museum

Paparigopoúlou 7 ⊛ www .athenscitymuseum.gr. Mon & Wed–Fri 9am–4pm, Thurs noon–8pm, Sat & Sun 10am–3pm. €3. The City of Athens Museum stands on Platía Klafthomónos which, partly thanks to cosmetic work in the run-up to the Olympics, itself offers something of an Athenian history lesson. There's a wonderful view up from the square towards three grand Neoclassical buildings on Panepistimíou. Here the planners' conceptualization of the capital of newly independent Greece can for once be seen more or less as they envisaged it, blending the nation's Classical heritage with modern, Western values. As you look up you see, from the left, the sober, grey marble of the National Library, the rather racier Akadhimía (University), enlivened by frescoes depicting King Otto surrounded by ancient Greek gods and heroes, and the frankly over-the-top Academy of Science with its pediment friezes and giant statues of Athena and Apollo.

PLACES

Platía Omonías and the bazaar

The garish decoration gives an alarming impression of what the Classical monuments might have looked like when their paintwork was intact.

The museum itself is housed in a mansion that was the residence of King Otto in the 1830s before his new palace was completed, and its exhibits cover Athens' history from Otto's time onwards. Some of the rooms have been restored to their state when the royals lived here, with exquisite period furnishings, and there are many artworks featuring the city as well as an interesting model of Athens in 1842, with just three hundred houses. A section of the ancient city walls can be seen in a basement.

Numismatic Museum

Panepistimíou 12. Tues–Sun 8.30am–3pm. €3. A collection of over 600,000 coins and related artefacts – weights, lead stamps, medals, precious stones and a rich archive of documents – dating from Mycenaean times through Classical, Macedonian and Roman to Byzantine and the modern era. The building itself, the magnificent former home of the German archeologist Heinrich Schliemann (excavator of Troy and Mycenae), is a substantial part of the attraction.

Shops

To Biblio Ippo Tap

Panepistimíou 57, in the arcade. High-quality outlet for official archeological-service publications – including guides to many obscure sites – that also sells first-rate museum reproductions.

Eleftheroudhakis

Panepistimíou 17. Five floors of books provide space for an extensive stock, with plenty in

▼ LITTLE INDIA

English; there's also an Internet café and an excellent cafeteria with a large selection of vegetarian dishes and sweets.

Eteria Hatzidhimia

Evripídhou 32. Wonderfully old-fashioned liquor store with dozens of types of ouzo, brandy and wines.

Hondos Centre

Platía Omonías 4. The city's top department store; though it's definitely no Harrods – low-ceilinged, cramped and crowded – the Hondos Centre is reasonably priced and stocks just about everything you could want. It has several floors of clothes, as well as a top-floor café with Acropolis views.

Ikologi Elladas (The Ecological Café)

Panepistimíou 57 ⊛ www.oikologoi .gr. A tremendously well-stocked health-food store and vegetarian cafeteria/juice bar with a pleasant loft where afternoon treats are served.

Lesvos

Athinás 33. Very different from the traditional shops around the nearby market, this glossy and somewhat touristy deli sells high-quality wine, honey, preserves and olive oil as well as bread, cheese and meats.

Nazca

Eólou 89. Five floors of outdoor gear, from high-fashion T-shirts to ropes and crampons.

Notos Galleries, Lambropoulos

Eólou 99. One of Athens' oldest and biggest department stores, stocking clothes, household goods, sports gear and electrical items at reasonable prices.

▲ KIOSK, OMONÍA

PMW Records

Panepistimíou 66 & Patission 2. Music, DVDs, games and accessories on five floors.

Politeia

Asklipíou 1–3, cnr Akadhimías. Bookshop with three entrances from the street according to category, including an excellent, competitively-priced range in English.

Xylouris

Panepistimíou 39, in the arcade. Run by the widow of the late, great Cretan singer Nikos Xylouris, this is one of the best places for finding Greek popular, folk and Cretan music.

Cafés

Delphi Café

Ayíou Konstandínou 27, below the Delphi Art Hotel. A peaceful escape just a short way from Platía Omonías, with excellent coffee as well as hamburgers, omelettes, salads and sandwiches.

Krinos

Eólou 87, behind the central market. Operating since 1922, though thanks to recent refurbishment the only signs of that are the old photos adorning the walls. Still popular for old-fashioned treats like *loukoumádhes* (pastry puffs soaked in honey–citrus syrup and dusted in cinnamon) and *bougátsa*, as well as sandwiches and ice cream.

Themis

Platía Kótzia, cnr Apollon, opposite the Post Office. A truly old-fashioned *kafenío* – an almost forgotten institution in Athens – peopled almost exclusively by old men drinking traditional Greek coffee.

Restaurants

Andreas

Themistokléous 18 ☏ 210 38 21 522. Lunchtime Mon–Sat. Like the *Athinaïkon* (below), a traditional ouzerí that's popular for long weekday lunches.

Arkhaion Yefsis

Kodhrátou 22, Metaxouryío ☏ 210 52 39 661, ⊛ www.arxaion.gr. The name means "ancient tastes" and this highly original restaurant claims to serve ancient Greek food, based on evidence from contemporary writings. It certainly makes for an enjoyable evening, in a lovely if slightly tacky setting with bare stone walls, statues, flaming torches and a courtyard. Dishes include wild-boar cutlets and goat leg with mashed vegetables, cheese, garlic and honey, as well as plenty of less meaty options.

Athinaïkon

Themistokléous 2, cnr Panepistimíou ☏ 210 38 38 485. Closed Sun, closed Aug. Long-established, old-fashioned ouzerí with a huge variety of good-sized,

mid-priced *mezédhes*: seafood – such as shrimp croquettes and mussels simmered with cheese and peppers – is a speciality.

Dhiporto

Theátrou, cnr Sokrátous. Mon–Sat 6am–6pm. Two brown-painted metal trapdoors in the pavement open to a steep stairway down into a basement that feels like it survives from an Athens of fifty years ago. Simple, inexpensive Greek food – chickpea soup, Greek salad, fried fish – washed down with *retsina* is enjoyed by market workers as well as tourists and office suits, and, as the afternoon wears on, impromptu music often breaks out.

Doris

Praxitelous 30 ☏ 210 32 32 671. Mon–Sat 7.30am–6pm. A straightforward, reliable place that has been serving for decades. Famous for its *loukoumádhes* (pastry puffs soaked in syrup), but also serves grills and baked dishes.

Guru

Platía Theátrou 10 ☏ 210 32 46 530. High-fashion Thai restaurant plus late-night bar/club, whose artistically rusty iron facade is utterly out of keeping with the ugly concrete office-blocks roundabout. Given the setting, the food is surprisingly authentic and not too pricey.

Ideal

Panepistimíou 46 ☏ 210 33 03 000. Closed Sun. A staunch city-centre establishment favoured by middle-class Greeks – especially at lunchtime – for its clubby, Art Nouveau atmosphere. Swish and slightly old-fashioned – *schnitzel* and chops – but the mid-priced menu also includes twenty or more fresh daily specials.

▲ KLIMATARIA

Klimataria

Platía Theátrou 2 ☎ 210 32 16 629. Lunchtimes plus Fri & Sat eve. Friendly, old-fashioned taverna serving ample portions of traditional fare at reasonable prices. Take a look at the daily specials in the kitchen; there are usually excellent vegetable dishes plus daily roast meats. Barrels of wine are just about the only decoration, but there's open courtyard seating in summer and live music at the end of the week.

Lefteris

Satovriándhou 20 ☎ 210 52 25 676. Hole-in-the-wall *souvláki* place that also serves simple grills – good for a quick lunch; the draft wines are very good.

Nargis

Sofokléous 60 ☎ 210 52 48 095. Tucked inside a tiny *stoa*, this small, basic Bengali canteen wins no prizes for decor, but has an authentic Indian atmosphere and meat and vegetarian curries at very low prices.

Pak Indian

Menándhrou 13 ☎ 210 32 19 412. Handsomely decorated Indian restaurant, somewhat at odds with its surroundings. The food is excellent – fresh and delicately spiced, and there's interesting taped music, as well as the occasional live performance.

Live music

Elatos

Trítis Septemvríou 16 ☎ 210 52 34 262. Closed Wed. An eclectic assortment of *dhimotiká* in this traditional, downtown basement club.

Laba

Víktoros Ougó 22, cnr Akominátou, Metaxouryío ☎ 210 52 28 188. Big, central rebétika place that can attract big names. Drinks €10.

Rodon

Márni 24, Platía Váthis ☎ 210 52 47 427. Closed in summer. Converted cinema that hosts foreign and Greek indie, rock, soul and reggae groups – in an intimate atmosphere.

Stoa Athanaton

Sofokléous 19 ☎ 210 32 14 362. 3–6pm & midnight–6am; closed Sun & May–Aug. Rebétika-place fronted by *bouzoúki* veterans Hondronakos and company. Good taverna food at reasonable prices, but drinks are expensive.

The Archeological Museum, Exárhia and Neápoli

In northern Athens there's just one "sight" of any note, and it is an essential stop on any visit to Athens, however brief. The fabulous National Archeological Museum is simply the finest collection of ancient Greek artefacts anywhere, and regarded as among the top ten museums in the world. However high your expectations, the museum seems effortlessly to surpass them, full of objects that seem familiar, so often have you seen them in pictures or reproductions.

There are few specific sights otherwise, but it's a rewarding part of the city for a wander – restaurants, bars, cafés and bookshops abound. Exárhia, fifty-odd blocks squeezed between the National Archeological Museum and Lófos tou Stréfi, is one of the city's liveliest neighbourhoods, especially at night. Traditionally the home of anarchists, revolutionaries, artists, students and anyone seeking an anti-establishment lifestyle in a conformist city, Exárhia is pretty tame these days, but it's still the closest thing in central Athens to an "alternative" neighbourhood. Nearby Neápoli is home to a swathe of good, low-key tavernas, many featuring rebétika-style atmosphere and sometimes the music itself.

Just above this, the little-visited Stréfis Hill (Lófos tou Stréfi) provides some great views and a welcome break from the densely packed streets and dull apartment blocks surrounding it.

Polytekhnío Patission 42
The Neoclassical building housing the Polytechnic

▼ EXÁRHIA SQUARE

(Polytekhnío), the university's school of engineering and science is not open to visits, but it played a significant role in recent Greek history. In November 1973 students here launched a protest against the repressive regime of the colonels' junta, occupying the building and courtyards. In response, snipers fired indiscriminately into the protestors. Even today, nobody knows how many unarmed students were killed – estimates range from twenty to three hundred. The anniversary of the massacre is still commemorated by marches and sombre remembrance celebrations.

National Archeological Museum

Patission 44. ⊛ www.culture.gr. Summer Mon 1–7.30pm, Tues–Sun 8.30am–7.30pm; winter Mon 10.30am–5pm, Tues–Sun 8.30am–3pm. €7. The National Archeological Museum is an unrivalled treasure-house of ancient Greek art. The biggest crowd-pullers are the Mycenaean Halls, directly ahead of you as you enter, including the gold funerary mask of Agamemnon and large quantities of other gold jewellery and intricate objects from the fifteenth and fourteenth centuries BC. Other highlights here include a golden-horned Bull's Head displayed alongside a gold Lion's Head; gold jewellery including a diadem and a gold-foil cover for the body of an infant from Grave III (the "Grave of the Women"); the Acropolis Treasure of gold goblets, signet rings and jewellery; and dozens of examples of the Mycenaeans' consummate art, intricate, small-scale decoration of rings,

cups, seals and inlaid daggers. There's work in silver, ivory, bronze and boars' tusks as well; there are baked tablets of Linear B, the earliest Greek writing (mainly accounting records) and Cretan-style frescoes depicting chariot-borne women watching spotted hounds in pursuit of boar and bull-vaulting.

Still-earlier Greece is represented in the adjoining rooms. Room 5 covers Neolithic pottery and stone tools from Attica and elsewhere and runs through to the early Bronze Age. The pottery shows sophisticated decoration from as early as 5000 BC, and there are many figurines, probably fertility symbols judging by their phallic or pregnant nature, as well as simple gold ornaments. Room 6 is home to a large collection of **Cycladic** art from the Aegean islands. Many of these idols suggest the abstract forms of modern Cubist art – most strikingly in the much-reproduced *Man Playing a Lyre*.

The largest part of the collection, though, is sculpture, following a broadly chronological arrangement in a clockwise direction around the main halls of the museum. Early highlights include a statue of a kore (maiden) from Merenda (Myrrhinous) in Attica, in room 11. Nearby is a wonderful grave stele of a young *doryphoros* (spear-bearer) standing against a red background. Room 13 has the stele of a young warrior, with delicately carved beard, hair and tunic-folds.

Of the massive **Classical collection** the bronzes stand out: in particular the Statue of Poseidon, poised to throw his trident, and the Little Jockey of Artemission, both of them recovered from a wreck off

PLACES

The Archeological Museum, Exárhia and Neápoli

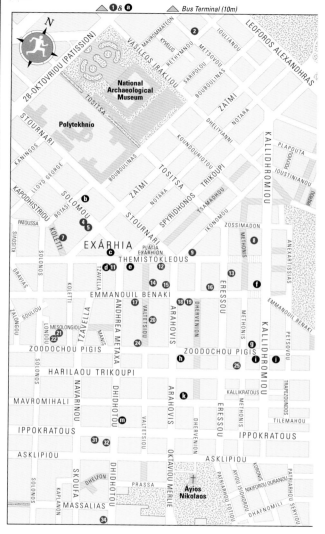

Évvia in the 1920s; near it in room 21 is the Atalante Hermes, a wonderful funerary statue of a youth. Room 28 has some fine, fourth-century-BC bronzes including the Antikithira Youth, thought to

depict either Perseus or Paris, from yet another shipwreck, off Antikithira, and the bronze head of a Boxer, burly and battered.

Less visited, but still extremely worthwhile, are the collections

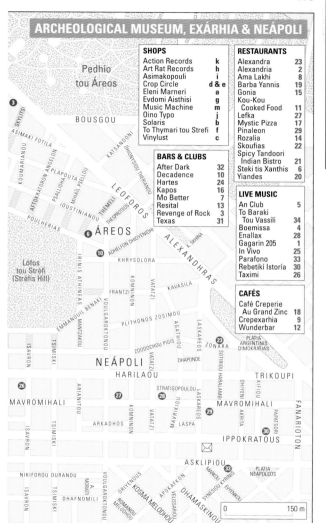

ARCHEOLOGICAL MUSEUM, EXÁRHIA & NEÁPOLI

Pedhío tou Áreos

BOUSGOU

SHOPS

Action Records	**k**
Art Rat Records	**h**
Asimakopouli	**i**
Crop Circle	**d & e**
Eleni Marneri	**a**
Evdomi Aisthisi	**g**
Music Machine	**m**
Oino Typo	**j**
Solaris	**b**
To Thymari tou Strefi	**f**
Vinylust	**c**

BARS & CLUBS

After Dark	32
Decadence	10
Hartes	24
Kapos	16
Mo Better	7
Resital	13
Revenge of Rock	3
Texas	31

RESTAURANTS

Alexandra	23
Alexandria	2
Ama Lakhi	8
Barba Yannis	19
Gonia	15
Kou-Kou Cooked Food	11
Lefka	27
Mystic Pizza	17
Pinaleon	29
Rozalia	14
Skoufias	22
Spicy Tandoori Indian Bistro	21
Steki tis Xanthis	6
Yiandes	20

LIVE MUSIC

An Club	5
To Baraki Tou Vassili	34
Boemissa	4
Enallax	28
Gagarin 205	1
In Vivo	25
Parafono	33
Rebetiki Istoría	30
Taximi	26

CAFÉS

Café Creperie Au Grand Zinc	18
Crepexarhia	9
Wunderbar	12

Lófos tou Stréfi (Stréfis Hill)

NEÁPOLI

HARILAOU

TRIKOUPI

MAVROMIHALI

MAVROMIHALI

IPPOKRATOUS

ASKLIPIOU

PLATIA NEAPOLEOS

0   150 m

PLACES   The Archeological Museum, Exárhia and Neápoli

of bronze-work – at the rear of the museum – and vases – upstairs. Also upstairs is a room devoted to the excavations at Thirá (Santorini), where some of the famous frecoes discovered there are displayed.

Lófos tou Stréfi (Stréfis Hill)

Overlooking Neápoli, the little-visited Stréfis Hill (Lófos tou Stréfi) rises above the residential streets that surround it. A labyrinth of paths leads up to the low summit, from

▲ GROUNDS OF THE POLYTEKHNÍO

where there are unexpectedly wonderful views – above all of the Acropolis with the Saronic Gulf and islands behind, but also across to nearby Lykavitós. Watch out for unguarded drops near the top and stick to the main paths as you walk up to avoid one of the more obvious signs of the area's alternative lifestyle, discarded hypodermics.

Pedhío tou Áreos

One of the few green areas in the centre of Athens, the Pedhío tou Áreos (Plain of Mars) is a substantial park of trees, gardens and meandering paths. A long boulevard bisects the park, with a line of statues of heroes of the Greek War of Independence keeping silent vigil over the strolling visitors.

Shops

Street markets

The local street market takes place over Kallidhromíou, between Exárhia Square and Lófos Stréfi, every Saturday.

Action Records

Mavromiháli 51. While you can find all the latest Greek and non-Greek CDs at the major retail stores on Stadhíou or Panepistimíou, this is the place to buy a genuine *bouzoúki*, *baglamás* or *laoúto* if you fancy your hand at playing Greek music.

Art Rat Records

Zoodóchou Piyís 48. A pocket-sized gem dealing exclusively in classic and progressive rock.

Asimakopouli

Hariláou Trikoúpi 82. One of the best patisseries in the city, offering a rich variety of fresh, high-quality sweets, cakes, home-made ice cream and excellent *tsoureki* (sweet bread).

Crop Circle

Themistokléous 52 & 66. Reasonably priced vintage clothing and ethnic jewellery. The branch higher up the hill sells new stock, the lower one vintage.

Eleni Marneri

Agathoupóleos 3, Kypséli (off 28 Oktovríou, north of Metro Viktorías). A beautiful, contemporary jewellery shop whose decor reflects the innovative style of the various designers. A great selection and occasional exhibitions.

Evdomi Aisthisi

Hariláou Trikoúpi 77. Gifts on a Greek-island theme, with well-crafted ornaments, ceramics and papier-maché items.

Music Machine

Dhiodótou 16. Packed full of old vinyl albums of every genre; also deals in Hi-End.

Oino Typo

Hariláou Trikoúpi 98. Excellent wine merchant with over 50 varieties of Greece's famous barrelled wines, as well as 1200 international bottled wines.

Solaris

Botási 6. Comics – old and new – as well as science fiction.

To Thymari tou Strefi

Kallidhromíou 51. Traditional Greek produce (honey, herbs, cheese, olive oil and dried goods) in a quaint little store on Exárhia's most picturesque street. Get there for Saturday-morning's fruit and vegetable market and enjoy the spectacle from one of the street's cafés.

Vinylust

Themistokléous 49. Rare albums, CDs, videos, DVDs and posters.

Cafés

Café Creperie Au Grand Zinc

Emmanouíl Benáki 88. The cosy, quiet, wood-lined interior makes a peaceful stop for coffee and crêpes.

Crepexarhia

Platía Exarhíon, cnr Themistokléous and Ikonómou. Simple crêperie in a busy corner of the square, also serving coffee, sandwiches and ice cream.

Wunderbar

Themistokléous 80, Platía Exarhíon. Something for everyone here: a café by day, with tables out on the square, bar in the evening, and late-night clubbing to electro and techno-pop sounds.

Restaurants

Alexandra

Zonará 21, off Leofóros Alexandhrás ☎210 64 20 874. Closed Sun. Obscure location, but this modernized mansion has smart decor, a verandah in summer, and occasional accordion music. The food is imaginative and not too pricey: aubergine croquettes, beetroot salad with walnuts, and meat in various sauces.

Alexandria

Metsóvou 13, cnr Rethýmnou ☎210 82 10 004. Mon–Sat, eves only; closed Aug. Middle-Eastern food with an Egyptian theme – palms and ceiling fans – and a pleasant courtyard garden. Booking advised.

Ama Lakhi

Kallidhromíou 69 or Methónis 66 ☎210 38 45 978. A fine old mansion with a huge courtyard where tables are set out in summer: entry to the house from Kallidhromíou, to the courtyard from Methónis. The food is good-value, traditional taverna fare.

Barba Yannis

Emmanouíl Benáki 94 ☎210 33 00 185. Popular neighbourhood treasure with a varied menu of home-style oven food (changes daily and displayed in large pots near entrance) in a relaxed atmosphere, aided and abetted by barrelled wine. Tables outside on pedestrianized street in summer. Open all day until the small hours.

Gonia

Arahóvis 59. Mushroom *saganáki*, meatballs, spicy sausages and octopus are among the delights at this basic, old-fashioned ouzerí.

Kou-Kou Cooked Food
Themistokléous 66 ☏ 210 38 31 955. Mon–Sat; closed mid-Aug.
Just off Platía Exarhíon, this inexpensive, modern, café-style place serves traditional dishes like *tsoutsoukákia* (meatballs in tomato sauce), as well as more modern Greek food. Menu in Greek only.

Lefka
Mavromiháli 121 ☏ 210 36 14 038. Closed Sun. Beloved old taverna with great *fáva* (hummus-like bean purée), black-eyed beans and baked and grilled meat with barrelled *retsina*. Summer seating in a huge garden enclosed by barrels.

Mystic Pizza
Emmanouíl Benáki 76, Exárhia ☏ 210 38 39 500. Tiny, unpretentious place serving pasta and salads as well as excellent, inexpensive pizzas. Takeaway and delivery service too.

Pinaleon
Mavromiháli 152 ☏ 210 64 40 945. Closed in summer, June–Sept.

▼ ROZALIA

A classic ouzerí-style establishment, serving rich *mezédhes* and meaty entrées, washed down with home-made wine, lovingly brewed by the chef/owner from Híos. Advance booking is recommended.

Rozalia

Valtetsíou 58 ☎ 210 33 02 933. Ever-popular mid-range taverna, with excellent chicken and highly palatable barrelled wine. You order *mezédhes* from the tray as the waiters thread their way through the throng; also a regular menu of grilled fish and meat. In summer you can dine in the garden opposite.

Skoufias

Lóndou 4 ☎ 210 38 28 206. Well-known taverna that has relocated to this busy pedestrian alley; bar atmosphere but good food too.

Spicy Tandoori Indian Bistro

Messolongíou 4. Simple but authentic curry-house livening up the tastebuds of Exárhia with *bhunas*, *biryanis* and *vindaloos*.

Steki tis Xanthis

Irínis Athinéas 5 ☎ 210 88 20 780. Closed Sun. A delightful old mansion at the base of Lófos Stréfi with a roof garden that offers fine views: approach from the hill, or up steep steps from Leofóros Alexandhrás. House specialities from a traditional menu include rabbit stew and *schnitzel*.

Yiandes

Valtetsíou 44 ☎ 210 33 01 369. Modern and, for Exárhia, upmarket restaurant serving excellent food that's based on a modern take on Greek cuisine with Asian influences. Pleasant courtyard.

Bars & clubs

After Dark

Dhiodótou 31 & Ippokrátous ☎ 210 36 06 460. From 10pm. €5 entry. Rock, blues and soul, plus the occasional live performance by Greek indie bands to a young crowd.

Decadence

Voulgaroktónou 69 & Poulherías ☎ 210 88 27 045. Opens 11pm. Popular with students, classic underground rock reverberates until late, while you can also catch some independent rock and electronic pop, and some live performances. Theme nights as varied as "Viva Espana" to a Cure tribute.

Hartes

Valtetsíou 35, cnr Zoodóchou Piyís ☎ 210 33 04 778. A crowded, early-evening meeting place, this café-bar has a great location for people watching from its outdoor tables. Good rock music too.

Kapos

Emmanouíl Benáki 87. Bar-café housed in an old mansion with numerous rooms featuring different musical vibes plus a pleasant courtyard.

Mo Better

Kolétti 32 ☎ 210 38 12 981. €6 entry includes drink. Cramped but fun bar on the first floor of a Neoclassical building. Hip-hop, garage, punk and indie rock with resident DJ.

Resital

Eressoú 64 ☎ 210 38 05 556. One of the longest-established music bars in Exárhia. The club is upstairs in an ivy-draped mansion, with over-the-top decor, live Greek and rock sounds, plus a roof terrace to escape it all.

Revenge of Rock

Leofóros Alexandhrás 34, opposite Pedhío Áreos Park ☎ 210 88 30 695. Large club with classic and hard rock sounds and occasional live performances.

Texas

Ippokrátous 56 ☎ 6972 802 171, ⓦ www.texasclub.gr. Heavy-metal bar also catering to goth and glam rockers; Western theme, loud music, party atmosphere.

Live music

An Club

Solomoú 13–15 ☎ 210 33 05 056. From 10pm. €10 entry. Basement club featuring live performances by local and lesser-known foreign rock-bands.

To Baraki tou Vassili

Dhidhótou 3 ☎ 210 36 23 625, ⓦ www.tobaraki.gr. €15 entry includes first drink. Daily acoustic performances: a showcase for up-and-coming rebétika acts and popular singer-songwriters.

Boemissa

Solomoú 19 ☎ 210 38 43 836. Tues–Sun 11pm–4am. Reservations recommended. Rebétika and laïká place popular with university students, who jam the dance floor and aisles, and inevitably end up writhing on the tabletops as well. Good company of musicians play music from all regions of Greece. Drinks €7: two-drink minimum; *mezédhes* served.

Enallax

Mavromiháli 139 ☎ 210 64 37 416. No cover charge, but reservation essential. Lively, friendly venue hosting Greek folk acts; drinks from €8. Live gigs mostly Thurs–Sat.

Gagarin 205

Liossíon 205, near Metro Attikís ☎ 210 85 47 601, ⓦ www.gagarin205.gr. A long way north, but probably the finest venue for live rock in Athens, where some 2000 fans can crowd in to see the best touring indie bands as well as local talent and club nights. In summer, the action moves down to Fáliro, on the coast, and *Gagarin on the Beach*.

In Vivo

Harilaóu Trikoúpi 79 ☎ 210 38 22 103. From 10pm, entry €6. Blues, jazz and rock at a reliable venue open through the summer.

Parafono

Asklipíou 130a ☎ 210 64 46 512. Excellent jazz and blues – mainly local groups – in a congenial, small, cabaret-style club.

Rebetiki Istoria

Ippokrátous 181 ☎ 210 64 24 937. Closed Wed & July–Aug. A lovely old house with traditional rebétika sounds from a good company; drinks from €6, and tasty food is also served.

Taximi

Isávron 29 ☎ 210 36 39 919. Closed Sun & July–Aug. This large, crowded rebétika salon on the third floor of a Neoclassical building seems to have been around for ever. It attracts a crowd of all ages; no cover, but drinks from €7 and pricey *mezédhes* available.

Kolonáki and Lykavitós Hill

If you have money to spend, Kolonáki is the place to do it, catering as it does to every Western taste from fast food to high fashion. It's also from here that a funicular hauls you up Lykavitós Hill, where some of the best views of the city can be enjoyed. Close at hand, too, is a clutch of major museums.

The Museum of Cycladic Art, the eclectic Benáki collection and the Byzantine and Christian Museum are particularly worthwhile; the War Museum and National Gallery of Art of more specialist interest. Near the latter, what are believed to be the fourth-century-BC foundations of Aristotle's Lyceum – where he taught for thirteen years and to which Socrates was a frequent visitor – were recently unearthed. Surrounded by museums, this seems an appropriate place for it, but important as the discovery is for scholars, there's nothing actually to see.

At night the area is at its liveliest, with plenty of upmarket bars, cafés and restaurants. Further east, the more modern areas of Ilísia and Ambelókipi have more good bars and music clubs, as well as the Mégaro Mousikís, Athens' principal concert hall.

Kolonáki

Kolonáki is the city's most chic central address and shopping area. Walk up from Sýndagma, past the jewellery stores on Voukourestíou, and you can almost smell the money. The neighbourhood's lower limits are defined by Akadhimías and Vasilíssis Sofías streets, where grand Neoclassical palaces house embassies and museums. The middle stretches of the quarter are taken up with shops, while the highest, wonderfully located on the southwest-facing slopes of Lykavitós, looking out over the Acropolis and National Gardens, are purely residential.

The heart of it all is a square officially called Platía Filikís Eterías, but known to all as

▼ KOLONÁKI

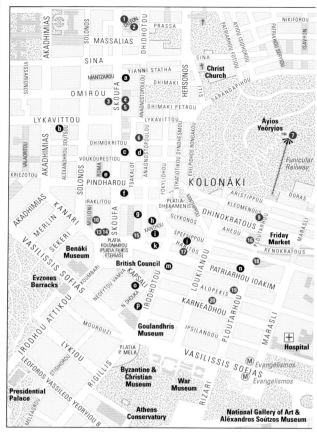

RESTAURANTS			
Altamira	6	To Kotopoulo	13
Dhimokritos	6	Kriti	21
Filippou	16	Orizontes Lycavitou	7
Ikio	19	Ouzadikou	20
Jackson Hall	10	Ouzerí	9
To Kioupi	14	Il Postino	2

BARS AND CLUBS			
Baila	18	Memphis	24
Balthazar	11	Mike's Irish Bar	22
Café Alu	3	Mommy	1
Craft	12		

Platía Kolonakíou, after
the ancient "little column"
that hides in the trees on the
southwest side. Dotted around
the square are kiosks with
stocks of foreign papers and
magazines, or in the library of
the **British Council** you can
check out the British press for
free. The surrounding cafés are
almost invariably packed with
Gucci-clad shoppers – you'll
find better value if you move
away from the square a little.
In the dozens of small,
upmarket **shops** the accent is

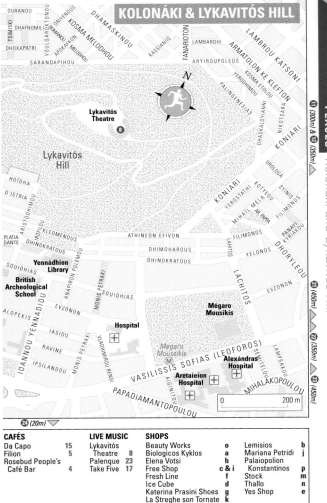

CAFÉS		LIVE MUSIC		SHOPS			
Da Capo	15	Lykavitós		Beauty Works	**o**	Lemisios	**b**
Filion	5	Theatre	8	Biologicos Kyklos	**a**	Mariana Petridi	**j**
Rosebud People's		Palenque	23	Elena Votsi	**h**	Palaiopolion	
Café Bar	4	Take Five	17	Free Shop	**c & i**	Konstantinos	**p**
				Fresh Line	**f**	Stock	**m**
				Ice Cube	**d**	Thallo	**n**
				Katerina Prasini Shoes	**g**	Yes Shop	**e**
				La Streghe son Tornate	**k**		

firmly on fashion and designer gear, and a half-hour stroll around the neighbourhood will garner the whole gamut of consumer style.

For more random strolling, the highest tiers of Kolonáki can be very enjoyable, with steep streets ending in long flights of steps, planted with oleander and jasmine.

Lykavitós Hill

Lykavitós Hill offers tremendous views, particularly from late afternoon onwards – on a clear

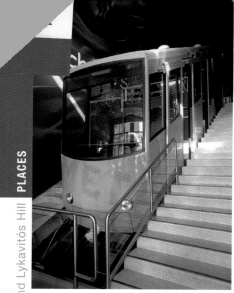

▲ FUNICULAR

a climb – though it doesn't look far from Kolonáki square, it's a steep ascent through the stepped residential streets. To do the whole journey the lazy way take bus #060 to the base of the funicular – this starts its journey at the terminus beside the National Archeological Museum and has handy stops on Akadhimías.

The principal path up the hill begins from the western end of Aristípou above Platía Dhexamenís, rambling through woods to the top. It's not as long or as hard a walk as it looks – easily done in twenty minutes – though the top half offers little shade.

day you can see the mountains of the Peloponnese. After dark, the shimmering lights of Athens spread right across the Attica basin. To get to the summit you can take the funicular (daily 9am–3am; every 30min, more frequent at busy times; €4.50 return) or you can walk. The funicular begins its ascent from Odhós Aristípou, near the top of Ploutárhou. To get here is in itself something of

On the summit, the brilliantly white chapel of **Áyios Yeóryios** dominates – a spectacular place to celebrate the saint's name-day (April 24) if you're in Athens at the time. Just below it, *Orizontes* (p.128) is a very expensive restaurant with an equally expensive café, both of

▼ ÁYIOS YEÓRYIOS CHAPEL

which enjoy spectacular views. Over to the east a second, slightly lower peak is dominated by the open-air **Lykavitós Theatre**, which is used mainly for concerts from May to October. There's a road up to the theatre, and if you head down in this direction you emerge in Kolonáki near the lovely little enclave that the British and American archeological schools have created for themselves on Odhós Souidhías.

The Benáki Museum

Koumbári 1, cnr Vasilíssis Sofías ⓦ www.benaki.gr. Mon, Wed, Fri & Sat 9am–5pm, Thurs 9am–midnight, Sun 9am–3pm. €6, temporary exhibitions €3. The often overlooked but fascinating Benáki Museum should not be missed. Housing a private collection donated to the state in the 1950s by Antonis Benákis, a wealthy cotton merchant, exhibits range from Mycenaean jewellery, Greek costumes and folk artefacts to memorabilia from Byron and the Greek War of Independence, as well as jewellery from the Hélène Stathatos collection.

More than twenty thousand items are exhibited chronologically; ancient finds are on the lower floors and the modern Greek artefacts on the upper floors. Among the more unusual items are collections of early Greek Gospels, liturgical vestments and church ornaments rescued by Greek refugees from Asia Minor in 1922. There are also dazzling embroideries and body ornaments, and some unique material on Cretan

▲ CYCLADIC MUSEUM

independence and its architect, the statesman Elefthérios Venizélos, as well as on the Asia Minor crisis. An additional attraction, especially if you've been dodging traffic all day, is the pricey rooftop café, with views from the verandah over the nearby National Gardens. The museum shop stocks a fine selection of books on Greek folk art, CDs of regional music, and some of the best posters and postcards in the city.

Goulandhrís Museum of Cycladic and Ancient Greek Art

Neofýtou Dhouká 4 ⓦ www.cycladic-m.gr. Mon, Wed, Thurs & Fri 10am–4pm, Sat 10am–3pm. €3.50. The small, private Goulandhrís Museum of Cycladic and Ancient Greek Art is a beautifully presented collection that includes objects from the Cycladic civilization (third millennium BC, from the islands of the Cyclades group),

▲ BYZANTINE ART

is the superb black–figure pottery, especially a collection of painted Classical-era bowls, often showing two unrelated scenes on opposite sides – for example, one of the star exhibits depicts revellers on one face and three men in cloaks conversing on the other. Others include, on the second floor, a depiction of Hephaistos' return to Olympus, with Hephaistos and Dionysos riding donkeys, and, on the top floor, a lovely *pyxis* with a lid of four horses.

On the ground floor and basement there's a tiny children's area and a good **shop**, as well as a pleasant **café** (with good vegetarian choices) in an internal courtyard. From here a covered walkway connects to the nineteenth-century **Stathatos House**, magnificently restored as an extension for temporary exhibitions.

pre-Minoan Bronze Age (second millennium BC) and the period from the fall of Mycenae to around 700 BC, plus a selection of Archaic, Classical and Hellenistic pottery.

The **Cycladic objects** are on the first floor – above all distinctive marble bowls and folded-arm figurines (mostly female) with sloping wedge heads whose style influenced twentieth-century artists like Moore, Picasso and Brancusi. The exact purpose of the effigies is unknown but, given their frequent discovery in grave-barrows, it's possible that they were spirit-world guides for the deceased, substitutes for the sacrifice of servants and attendants, or representations of the Earth Goddess. Their clean, white simplicity is in fact misleading, for they would originally have been painted. Look closely, and you can see that many still bear traces.

Of the **ancient Greek art** on the upper floors, the highlight

Byzantine and Christian Museum

Vasilíssis Sofías 22. Tues–Sun 8.30am–7.30pm. €4. The Byzantine and Christian Museum was completely refurbished in 2004, and they did a wonderful job. Excellently displayed in a beautiful building its collection is far more wide-ranging than you might expect from the name. The setting is a peaceful, courtyarded villa that once belonged to the Duchesse de Plaisance, an extravagantly eccentric French-American philhellene and widow of a Napoleonic general who helped fund the War of Independence.

The exhibits start with art from the very earliest days of

Christianity, whose fish and dove motifs can't disguise their extremely close parallels with Classical Greek objects. There are displays on everyday Byzantine life; reconstructions of parts of early churches (mosaic floors and chunks of masonry, some even from the Christian Parthenon); a Coptic section with antique clothing such as leather shoes decorated with gold leaf; and tombs in some of which offerings were left, again a reminder of a pagan heritage. But the highlights are the icons, with the earliest being from the thirteenth and fourteenth centuries. There are dozens of lovely examples, many of them double-sided, some mounted to be carried in procession, and you can follow the development of their style from the simplicity of the earliest icons to the Renaissance-influenced selections from the sixteenth century. Alongside the icons are some fine frescoes, including an entire dome reconstructed inside the museum.

War Museum

Cnr Vasilíssis Sofías & Rizári 2. Tues–Sun 9am–2pm. Free. The only "cultural" endowment of the 1967–74 junta, the War Museum becomes predictably militaristic and right-wing as it approaches modern events: the Asia Minor campaign, Greek forces in Korea, and so on. One room devoted to Cyprus, in particular, has a virulently anti-Turkish message that seems extraordinary given current relations between the countries (it is also full of Cypriot antiquities, presumably to demonstrate the island's Greek heritage). However, the bulk of the collection consists of weaponry and uniforms, with a large collection of eighteenth- and nineteenth-century swords and handguns, and a particular concentration on the Second World War era. Earlier times are also covered with displays on changing warfare from Mycenae through to the Byzantines and Turks, and an array of models of the acropolises and castles of Greece, both Classical and medieval. Outside are artillery pieces and planes, including a full-scale model of the Daedalus, one of the first-ever military aircraft, which dropped bombs on Turkish positions in December 1912 during the Balkan Wars.

National Art Gallery and Aléxandros Soútsos Museum

Vasiléos Konstandínou 50. Mon & Wed 9am–3pm & 6–9pm, Thurs–Sat 9am–3pm, Sun 10am–2pm. €6. The National Art Gallery – which is combined with the private collection of Athenian lawyer Aléxandros Soútsos – holds some 9500 paintings, sculptures and engravings as well as miniatures and furniture. Quantity, sadly, is not really matched by the quality of the exhibits.

The core collection is of Greek art from the sixteenth century to the present, and of the artists shown here only El Greco is well known outside Greece. One of the few modern painters to stand out is Nikos Hatzikyriakos-Ghikas (Ghika), well represented on the ground floor. On the mezzanine is a small group of canvases by the primitive painter Theophilos (more of whose work can be seen at the Museum of Greek Folk Art in Pláka – see p.68). Perhaps more interesting is the large temporary-exhibition space, often hosting major

▲ SHOPPING IN KOLONÁKI

travelling exhibitions; keep an eye out for posters or check in the *Athens News*.

Shops

Street markets

Weekly local street-markets are held every Friday on Xenokrátous in the heart of Kolonáki and on Dhragoúmi in Ilísia, as well as on Saturdays on Plakendías in Ambelókipi.

Beauty Works

Kapsáli & Neofýtou Dhoúka, Kolonáki ☎210 72 25 511. Favoured by Madonna and other celebrities, the Beauty Works cosmetics chain stocks all the classic brands.

Biologicos Kyklos

Skoufá 52. Organic produce with some perishable goods available, good for supplements and essential oils.

Elena Votsi

Xanthoú 7, Kolonáki. An amazing little shop that's home to Elena's internationally acclaimed innovative jewellery designs, wich incorporate precious and semiprecious stones as well as materials such as shells.

Free Shop

Háritos 8 and Voukourestíou 50, Kolonáki. Own-label clothes, designed in Athens, including unisex tracksuits and T-shirts. These are sold mainly at the Háritos branch, while the Voukourestíou shop concentrates on international designers like Balenciaga.

Fresh Line

Skoufá 10. A must for lovers of fresh, homemade bath products made from Greek fruits, honey, herbs, flowers and essential oils.

Ice Cube

Tsakálof 28, Kolonáki. Beautiful designer boutique whose avant-garde designs are a welcome breath of fresh air. Attracts a young but deep-pocketed crowd. There's another branch in Glyfádha.

Katerina Prasini Shoes

Tsakálof 7. A small basement shoe-shop near the square where you can pick up Campers and other well-known brands, as well as bags, often at half price.

Lemisios

Lykavitoú 6, Kolonáki. Lemisios has been around since 1912. They mainly make leather sandals and ballet flats of a much better quality than the tourist versions on sale in Pláka and Monastiráki. They even do custom-made if you can wait two weeks: take material along with you and they will make shoes up with it.

Mariana Petridi

Háritos 34, Kolonáki. A showcase for Greek jewellery with varying styles, as well as work by Mariana Petridi herself.

Palaiopoleion Konstantinos

Irodótou 15. All sorts of antiques from jewellery to lamps and china from Greece and abroad.

Stock

Irodótou 24. This little boutique offers old-stock designer clothes and accessories at bargain prices.

Le Streghe son Tornate

Háritos 9, Kolonáki. One of the few vintage-clothes shops in Athens: mainly designer and top-end clothing, though, so few bargains.

Thallo

Plutarchou 25. This small jewellery shop is well worth a visit. Greek plants and flowers are coated in silver and gold to gorgeous effect and the prices are among the least intimidating in Kolonáki.

Yes Shop

Pindhárou 38, Kolonáki. A great little boutique with clothes by Greek designer Yióryios Eleftheriades, whose designs manage to be original and classic at the same time.

Cafés

Da Capo

Tsakálof 1, Kolonáki. A very popular establishment on this pedestrianized street, just north of Kolonáki square. *Da Capo* is very chic and, unusually, self-service.

Filion

Skoufá 34. A local institution for coffee, cakes, omelettes, salads and breakfast; busy at all times

▲ ALTAMIRA

PLACES Kolonáki and Lykavitós Hill

of day with a more sober crowd than the average Kolonáki café.

Rosebud People's Café Bar

Skoufá 40. One of a crowd of youth-oriented café-bars around the junction of Omírou: iced coffee by day; chilled sounds and DJs at night.

Restaurants

Altamira

Tsakálof 36A, Kolonáki ☎ 210 36 14 695. Multi-ethnic menu with Mexican, Indian, Asian and Arabic dishes – on the whole well done, and an interesting change from the usual Greek fare. The setting is lovely too, upstairs in an old mansion.

Dhimokritos

Dhimokrítou 23 ☎ 210 36 13 588. Closed Sun and August. Posh and perhaps a bit snooty – lots of suits at lunchtime – but a beautiful building and well-prepared, reasonably priced food from a vast menu, much of which is displayed in glass counters near the entrance.

Filippou

Xenokrátous 19 ☎ 210 72 16 390. Closed Sat eve & Sun. This old-time taverna, a favourite of local office workers and residents, is liveliest at lunchtime. Fresh food, moderately priced for the area, includes excellent traditional oven-baked dishes and casseroles.

Ikio

Ploútarhou 15 ☎ 210 72 59 216. The name means "homely", and that seems to be how the locals find it – a very busy, reasonably priced neighbourhood restaurant with a slightly modern take on Greek classics and a short menu of daily specials plus pasta and salads.

Jackson Hall

Milióni 4, Kolonáki ☎ 210 36 16 098. A very "Kolonáki" type of place; a big, busy, expensive American-themed diner with a music bar upstairs. Burgers, pasta, salads and the like.

To Kioupi

Platía Kolonakíou 4 ☎ 210 36 14 033. Closed Sun & Aug. Budget subterranean taverna with good, standard Greek fare such as *moussakás* and *dolmádhes*.

To Kotopoulo

Platía Kolonakíou, north side. Closed Sun. As the name indicates this tiny hole-in-the-wall is the place for chicken – juicy, crispy, rotisserie-style chicken, the best in Athens. It's strictly no-frills, lit by fluorescent lights and packed with people at all hours. A few tables on the pavement too, or take food away to eat in the nearby National Gardens or on the slopes of Lykavitós.

Kriti

Ayíou Thomá 18, off Michalakópoulou, Ambelókipi ☎ 210 77 58 258. Closed Mon. Very popular, simple ouzerí serving inexpensive Cretan-style food, often with live music.

Orizontes Lycavitou

Summit of Lykavitós Hill ☎ 210 72 10 701. Fabulous views from this glassed-in eyrie, or from its sheltered terrace. The prices are just as elevated, however, and the complex dishes (sea bass with green tagliatelle and Moschato wine sauce with peanuts, for example, at around €30) don't always live up to their promise.

Ouzadikou

Karneádhou 25–29 ☎ 210 72 95 484. Closed Sun & Mon. An unpromising setting in the lobby of a marble office building, but rightly popular with a middle-aged Kolonáki crowd for excellent *mezédhes*, some with a modern twist.

Ouzerí

Kleoménous 22, cnr Ploútarhou, just below the funicular. Nameless, simply furnished and very inexpensive ouzerí with salads and sandwiches as well as good, plain *mezédhes*.

Il Postino

Grivéon 3, in alleyway off Skoufá ☎ 210 36 41 414. Good-value modern Italian *trattoria*, serving freshly made pasta and simple Italian dishes in a friendly, bustling room.

Bars & clubs

Baila

Háritos 43 ☎ 210 72 33 019. Opens 12.30am. "Freestyle" sounds in this busy Kolonáki club, where an adjoining café-bar (*City*) offers a quieter alternative and outdoor tables.

Balthazar

Tsóha 27, Ambelókipi ☎ 210 64 12 300. Late-night meeting place of more mature, well-heeled clubbers, *Balthazar* has a wonderfully glamorous setting in an elegant mansion and its garden; restaurant earlier, cocktail bar with restrained sounds later.

Café Alu

Skoufá & Omírou 58 ☎ 210 36 11 116. Opens 10pm. Upbeat venue, hosting guest DJs playing mainly modern music.

Craft

Leofóros Alexándhras 205, Ambelókipi (right by Metro Ambelókipi) ☎ 210 64 62 350. Vast, modern microbrewery bar with half a dozen styles of in-house draught beer available in jugs, and giant-screen TVs for entertainment. Upstairs there's a Tex-Mex and Asian-themed restaurant.

Memphis

Vendíri 5, Ilisia, behind *Hilton Hotel* ☎ 210 72 24 104. Indie rock-bar with cool interior plus garden, and good sound-system blasting out rock and dance.

Mike's Irish Bar

Sinópis 6, Ambelókipi ☎ 210 77 76 797. In the shadow of the Athens Tower, a huge American-style basement bar with a young crowd and big screens for sporting events. Karaoke on Mondays and Tuesdays, live music most weekends.

Mommy

Delfón 4 ☎ 210 36 19 682. Opens 10pm. Something for everyone here – a bar/café/restaurant with good cocktails and fancy food (black risotto, Argentine steak) at fancy prices. Later on, soulful house is pumped out to thirty-somethings by resident DJs.

Live music

Lykavitós Theatre

Lykavitós Hill. Spectacular outdoor venue used mainly for music concerts from May to October.

Palenque

Farandáton 41, Platía Ayíou. Thomá, Ambelókipi ☎ 210 64 87 748. Live Latin music by South American groups, as well as salsa parties, flamenco music and dance lessons.

Take Five

Patriárkhou Ioakím 37 ☎ 210 72 40 736. Supper club with live jazz bands. Reservations advised. Tues–Wed & Fri–Sun.

Makriyiánni, Koukáki, Pangráti and Mets

South of the city centre, the neighbourhoods of Makriyiánni, Koukáki, Pangráti and Mets offer little in the way of sights, but each is full of character and home to excellent restaurants and cafés that see few tourists. Immediately south of the Acropolis, Makriyiánni is a decidely upmarket residential neighbourhood, merging into rather earthier Koukáki. There are numerous hotels here and good local eating places: no doubt the opening of the new Acropolis Museum in Makriyiánni (p.60) and the Contemporary Art Museum at Syngroú-Fix, on the fringes of Koukáki, will change things, but for the moment hardly any visitors come here other than those who are staying. Mets, a steep hillside area on the other side of busy Syngroú avenue, is a taste of old Athens. Here a few streets of pre-World War II houses survive almost intact: their tiled roofs, shuttered windows and courtyards with spiral metal staircases and potted plants, offering an intimate glimpse at the more traditional side of the city. The residential district of Pangráti, beyond, has a wealth of small, homely tavernas and *mezedhopolía*: Platía Plastíra, Platía Varnáva and Platía Pangratíou are the focal points, while Odhós Arhimídhous, off Platía Plastíra, holds an impressive street market every Friday.

Between Pangráti and Mets you'll also find the Panathenaic Stadium, which occupies an impressive spot next to Ardhittós Hill, and Athens' most prestigious cemetery, where lie the much-visited tombs of many of the country's luminaries.

The Panathenaic Stadium

The old Olympic Stadium or Panathenaic Stadium (aka Kalimármaro) is a nineteenth-century reconstruction on Roman foundations, slotted tightly in between the pine-covered spurs of Ardhittós Hill. You can't normally go inside, but you can go right up to the open end of its horsehoe shape, from where you get a very good view.

This site was originally marked out in the fourth century BC for the Panathenaic athletic contests, but in Roman times, as a grand gesture to mark the reign of the emperor

Visiting the area

All of these areas can be reached on **foot** from the centre – through the Záppio Gardens to Pangráti or Mets, south from Pláka or Thissío to Makriyiánni and Koukáki – but if you don't fancy the stroll you can hop on a #2, #4 or #11 trolley to Platía Plastíra in Pangráti and take the tram to the Panathenaic Stadium (Záppio stop) or use Akrópoli (Makriyiánni) or Syngroú-Fix (Koukáki) metro stations, or alternatively use trolleys #1 or #5, which run right through Makriyiánni and Koukáki.

Hadrian, it was adapted for an orgy of blood sports, with thousands of wild beasts baited and slaughtered in the arena. The Roman senator Herodes Atticus later undertook to refurbish the 60,000 seats of the entire stadium; the white marble from these was to provide the city with a convenient quarry through the ensuing seventeen centuries.

The stadium's reconstruction dates from the modern revival of the Olympic Games in 1896 and bears witness to the efforts of another wealthy benefactor, the Alexandrian Greek Yiorgos Averoff. Its appearance – pristine whiteness and meticulous symmetry – must be very much as it was when first restored and reopened under Herodes Atticus. Though the bends are too tight for major modern

events, it's still used by local athletes, is the finishing point of the annual Athens Marathon and lay at the end of the 2004 Olympic marathon.

Above the stadium to the south, on the secluded Hill of Ardhittós, are a few scant remnants of a Temple of Fortune, again constructed by Herodes Atticus.

The Próto Nekrotafío

The Próto Nekrotafío (First Cemetery) shelters the tombs of just about everybody who was anybody in nineteenth- and twentieth-century Greece, from archeologist Heinrich Schliemann to actress/activist Melina Mercouri and former prime minister Andreas Papandreou. The humbler tombs of musicians, artists and writers are interspersed with ornate

▼ THE OLYMPIC STADIUM

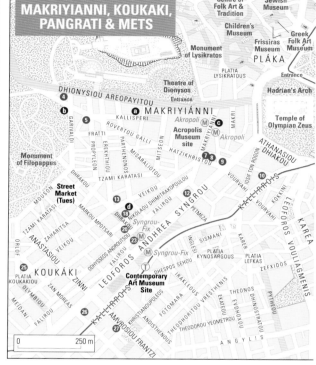

MAKRIYIANNI, KOUKAKI, PANGRATI & METS

RESTAURANTS						BARS AND CLUBS	
Ambrosia	23	Kalimarmaron	3	Spondi	22	Exo-Vitrine	6
Apanemia	13	Karavitis	2	Strofi	5	Granazi	7
Edodi	25	Mezedopolio Nota	14	Sushi Bar	19	Koukles	26
Ikositeseroöro	12	Mikri Vouli	17	Vyrinis	11	Lamda	9
Ilias	1	Pinelopi kai Mnistires	15			The Guys	8

mausoleums of soldiers, statesmen and wealthy families, whose descendants come to picnic, stroll and tend the graves. The graveside statuary occasionally attains the status of high art, most notably in the works of Ianoulis Halepas, a *Belle Époque* sculptor from Tínos generally acknowledged to be the greatest of a school of fellow-islanders. Halepas battled with mental illness for most of his life and died in extreme poverty in 1943;

his masterpiece is the idealized *Kimiméni* (Sleeping Girl), on the right about 300m in.

Shops

Street markets

There are local street-markets every Tuesday on Láskou in Pangráti, and every Friday on Tsámi Karatássou in Koukáki and Arhimídhous in Mets, behind the Panathenaic stadium.

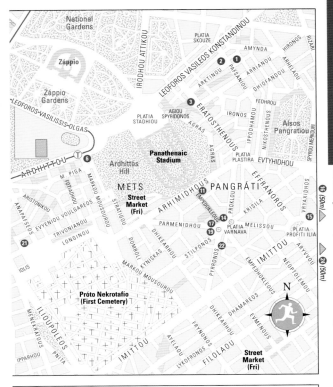

CAFÉS		LIVE MUSIC		SHOPS	
Diavlos Musiki Spiti	20	Alabastron	24	Greek Art	b
Dionysos Zonar's	4	Diavlos Musiki Spiti	20	Ilias Lalaounis Museum	a
Leonardo da Vinci	18	Half-Note	21	Stoa	c
		Pangratiotissa	16	Tsatsos	d
		Romeo	10		
		Stavros tou Notou	27		

Greek Art

Garibáldi 1 & Robérto Gálli, Makriyiánni. Good tourist place with souvenirs, postcards, T-shirts and other trinkets.

Ilias Lalaounis Museum

Kallispéri 12, Makriyiánni. Closed Tues. There is a museum displaying works by Ilias Lalaounis, founder of a world-renowned dynasty of goldsmiths, but also a jewellery workshop, museum shop and elegant bookstore. There's also a Lalaounis shop – fabulously expensive – at Panepistimíou 6 near Sýndagma.

Stoa

Makriyiánni 5, Makriyiánni. An arcade housing a number of interesting art and craft stores. Near the entrance are Art Shop, selling alternative jewellery and ceramics, and the tiny Trainotheatro art gallery and box office, where you can book theatre tickets for unique musical and theatrical productions, or buy vintage-style dolls or *objets d'art* on a railway theme – a real gem.

Tsatsos

Veïkou 45, Koukáki. Koukáki boasts some of the finest *zaharoplastía* (bakery/patisseries) in Athens, and *Tsatsos* is one of the best of them: try the traditional *kadaifi* and *baklava*.

Cafés

Diavlos Musiki Spiti

Dhrákou 9, Koukáki. Music club by night, but by day a really welcoming café with Greek sweets and snacks.

Dionysos Zonar's

Robérto Gálli 43, Makriyiánni. Traditional upmarket patisserie relocated to a modern building. The unbeatable position

▼ PANGRÁTI

opposite the Herodes Atticus Theatre is somewhat spoilt by being right above the main Acropolis coach park, and by the eye-watering prices. The complex also houses a pricey restaurant.

Leonardo da Vinci

Dhimitrakopoúlou 42, cnr Dhrákou, Koukáki. A reliable, all-purpose café: breakfast, frappés, ice cream, light meals, beer and wine. Seating indoors and out.

Restaurants

Ambrosia

Dhrákou 3–5, Koukáki ☎ 210 92 20 281. A friendly *psistariá* (grill house) packed with neighbourhood residents, especially on summer nights when the tables spill out into the pedestrian walkway. Food is simple but delicious – succulent grilled chicken, pork chops, kebabs and Greek salads – and service friendly and attentive. Many others nearby on this street.

Apanemia

Erekthíou 2 & Veïkou, Koukáki ☎ 210 92 28 766. Closed Sun. Basic, inexpensive *mezedhopolío* with a wide selection of authentic Mediteranean dishes as well as good menu of Greek standards.

Edodi

Veïkou 80, Koukáki ☎ 210 92 13 013. Eves only, closed Sun and all summer. Some say this is the finest restaurant in Athens, and if you want to splurge on exquisitely elaborate creations, this is the place to choose. Starters such as lobster-tail with spinach or *carpaccio* of smoked goose go for €15–20, mains like sea bass with lavender or chicken with sweet-potato curry around €25; fancy desserts too. Before you choose, the waiter will display everything to you, raw. Booking is essential.

Ikositeseroöro

Syngroú 42/44, Koukáki. The name means "24 hours", and that's its main virtue. Fair, if rather overpriced, portions of anti-hangover food such

▲ SPONDI

as lamb tongues and *patsás* at any time of day or night, in brightly lit, fast-food ambience. At its liveliest after midnight in summer.

Ilias

Stasínou, cnr Telesílis, Pangráti ☎210 72 15 155. Eves only. A very good, popular taverna with a standard menu and barrel wine. Tables outside in summer.

Kalimarmaron

Evforíonos 13 & Eratosthénous, Pangráti ☎210 70 19 727. Closed Mon & Sun. Smart taverna with a regularly changing menu featuring unusual old-fashioned dishes including some based on island recipes from Crete and Híos.

Karavitis

Arktínou 33, cnr Pafsaníou, Pangráti ☎210 72 15 155. Eves only. Old-style taverna with barrel wine, *mezédhes* and clay-cooked main courses. In summer there's outdoor seating in an enclosed garden.

Mezedopolio Nota

Platía Varnáva 9, Pangráti ☎210 70 15 169. Closed Sun. Small neighbourhood *mezedhopolío*, with tables out on the square in summer and live music most Friday and Saturday evenings. Excellent *meze*s, including some unusual varieties, and grilled meats.

Mikri Vouli

Platía Varnáva 8, Pangráti ☎210 75 65 523. Like its close neighbour *Nota*, a bustling local *mezedhopolío* with excellent traditional fare.

Pinelopi kai Mnistires

Imittoú 130 on Platía Profíti Ilía, Pangráti ☎210 75 68 555. Lively and bustling, "Penelope and her Suitors" is a friendly, elegant place with no-nonsense Greek food and regular live music.

Spondi

Pýrronos 5, Pangráti ☎ 210 75 20 658, ⓦ www.spondi.gr. Eves only. Long-time contender for the title of Athens' best restaurant, *Spondi* serves superb French-influenced cuisine, with fish a speciality. With starters – crab soup with ravioli scented with coriander, for example – from €25 and mains such as sea bass in fennel, olive oil and vanilla sauce or rabbit *provençal* starting at €30 it's not cheap, but for a special occasion it's worth it. Booking is essential.

Sushi Bar

Platía Varnáva, cnr Parménidhou, Pangráti ☎ 210 75 24 354. No surprises here – good-quality sushi, sashimi, and Japanese soups and salads.

Strofi

Robérto Gálli 25 ☎ 210 92 14 130, Makriyiánni. A comfortable, old-fashioned taverna serving classic Greek dishes like *stifado*, lamb with aubergine, or chops. Higher-than-average prices, but worth it for the roof terrace with great Acropolis views.

Vyrinis

Arhimídhous 11, Pangráti ☎ 210 70 12 153. Closed Sun. Classy taverna, recently redecorated in a modern style (prices increased to match, so slightly above average), with its own house wine and a wide variety of interesting *mezédhes*. Tables in a garden courtyard in summer.

Bars and clubs

Exo-Vitrine

Márkou Mousoúrou 1, Mets ☎ 210 92 37 109. Opens 9pm. €15 entrance Fri & Sat. A popular venue with the over-thirties, the balcony here has great views of Athens and Lykavitós by night. Café-bar earlier, at night transforms into a club with music from dance to mainstream.

Granazi

Lembési 20, Makriyiánni ☎ 210 92 13 054, ⓦ www.granazi.gr. This part of Makriyiánni was traditionally home to Athens' gay bars, and *Granazi* is one of numerous long-term survivors, generally attracting a more mature crowd than upstart rivals in Gázi. A chilled bar with videos and quiet music early on, getting louder as the night progresses. Mostly Greek music with shows at weekends.

The Guys

Lembési 8, Makriyiánni ☎ 210 92 14 244. Wed–Mon 10pm–3am. Greek and foreign music in a cool lounge-bar atmosphere draws a mature gay crowd.

Koukles

Zan Moreás 3, just off Syngroú, Koukáki ☎ 210 92 48 989. Wed–Sun only. The name means "Dolls" and the drag acts are said to be the best in Athens.

Lamda

Lembési 15, Makriyiánni ☎ 210 92 24 202, ⓦ www.lamdaclub.gr. Big, popular, late-night gay club with music ranging from house to Greek.

Live music

Alabastron
Damáreos 78, Pangráti ☎210 75 60 102. €6. Closed in summer.
Excellent atmosphere and live performances of a wide variety of music, from traditional jazz to African and Latin.

Diavlos Musiki Spiti
Dhrákou 9, Koukáki ☎210 92 39 588. Closed Mon, Tues & May–Sept.
Owned by the popular singer Yiannis Glezos, who sometimes puts in an appearance himself, the traditional music here ranges from rebétika to popular in style, with well-known performers often on the bill. The cover charge includes a drink, and on Thursday nights there are tango lessons followed by open dancing.

Half-Note
Trivonianoú 17, Mets ☎210 92 13 310. Closed Tues and much of the summer. Athens' premier jazz club, with live jazz most nights and frequent big-name touring performers.

Pangratiotissa
Zinodhótou 2, cnr Imittoú, Pangráti ☎210 75 19 475. Traditional neighbourhood place with nightly performances of rebétika and laïká: good *mezédhes* to enjoy while you listen.

Romeo
Kallíróis 4, Koukáki ☎210 92 24 885. Central *bouzoúkia*: glitzy, modern Greek music in a poppy atmosphere.

Stavros tou Notou
Tharípou 37, Neos Kosmos ☎210 92 26 975. One of the liveliest rock clubs in town; live shows mostly feature Greek artists but plenty of touring foreigners too.

Around Athens

Athens sprawls higher and wider each year and most of the places covered in this chapter, originally well outside the city, are now approached through a more or less continuous urban landscape. Nonetheless, they variously offer fresh air, seaside settings, and a change of pace from downtown Athens. The coastal suburbs, from Pireás to Glyfádha, are an essential summertime escape for Athenians, who head down here in droves: not just for beaches, but for cafés, restaurants, nightlife and shops. Thanks to the new tram it's easy to head down to the beach for a quick swim and be back in the centre just a couple of hours later; astonishingly, the water almost everywhere is clean and crystal clear. Pireás, meanwhile, has ferries to the islands, an excellent museum, and some of the best seafood in town.

Inland suburbs offer quieter attractions: **Kessarianí**, for example, whose monastery, still remarkably remote in feel, offers Byzantine architecture and a peaceful mountainside setting with opportunities for easy walking. **Kifissiá**, meanwhile, populated with expensive villas, provides an insight into wealthy Athenian life. Its relaxed combination of upmarket

shopping and café society, especially busy on Saturdays, can be combined with a visit to the Goulandhrís Natural History Museum and Gaia Centre.

Further afield, beyond the reach of the metro and city buses, **Attica** (Attikí), the region encompassing the capital, is not much explored by tourists – only the great romantic ruin of the Temple of Poseidon at

▼ PIREÁS FERRY

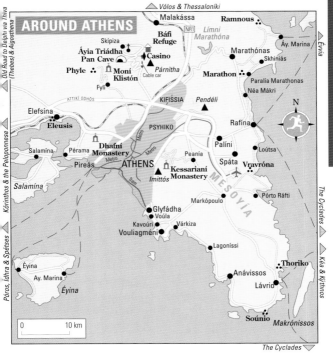

Cape Soúnio is at all well-known. Yet a trip out here makes for a pleasant break, with much of Greece in microcosm to be seen within an hour or two of the capital. There are rewarding archeological sites at **Eleusis** and **Ramnous** as well as at **Soúnio** and, if the heat is getting to you, plenty of beaches too. Combine a couple of these with a meal at one of the scores of seaside *psarotavernas* (fish restaurants), always packed out on summer weekends, and you've got a more than worthwhile day out.

Pireás

Pireás has been the port of Athens since Classical times,

Pireás transport

The metro takes about twenty minutes from Omonía to Pireás. You can also take the tram to SEF (the Stádhio Eirínis ké Fílias, or Peace and Friendship Stadium), the interchange with the metro at Néo Fáliro, which is in walking distance of Mikrolímano. Bus #40 (every 10min 5am–midnight, hourly 1–5am) runs between Pireás port and Sýndagma; #49 from Omonía (every 15min 5am–midnight, hourly 1–5am). Bus #904 runs from near the metro to Zéa Marina, trolley-bus #20 to Mikrolímano. Taxis cost around €8 at day-tariff from the centre of Athens – worth considering, especially if you're heading for Zéa Marina or Mikrolímano, which are a long walk from the metro.

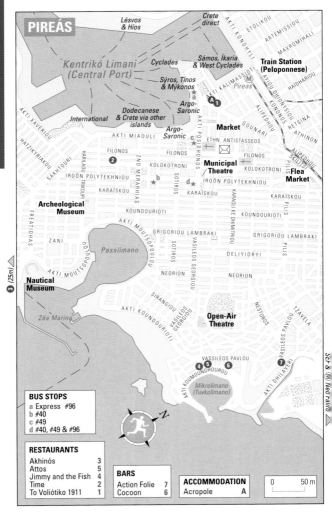

PIREÁS

Lésvos & Híos

Crete direct

Kentrikó Limani (Central Port)

Cyclades

Sámos, Íkaria & West Cyclades

Train Station (Peloponnese)

Pireas

Syros, Tinos & Mýkonos

Argo-Saronic

International

Dodecanese & Crete via other islands

Argo-Saronic

Market

AKTI MIAOULI

ETHN. ANTISTASSEOS

FILONOS

Municipal Theatre

Flea Market

FILONOS

KOLOKOTRONI

KOLOKOTRONI

IROÓN POLYTEKHNIOU

KARAÏSKOU

KARAÏSKOU

KARAÏSKOU

Archeological Museum

KOUNDOURIOTI

KOUNDOURIOTI

AKTI MOUTSOPOULOU

GRIGORIOU LAMBRAKI

GRIGORIOU LAMBRAKI

ZANI

Pasalímano

DELIYIORYI

AKTI MOUTSOPOULOU

NEORION

NEORION

Nautical Museum

Zéa Marina

AKTI KOUNDOURIOTI

Open-Air Theatre

VASSILEOS PAVLOU

Mikrolímano (Tuvkolímano)

BUS STOPS
a Express #96
b #40
c #49
d #40, #49 & #96

RESTAURANTS
Akhinós	3
Attos	5
Jimmy and the Fish	4
Time	2
To Voliótiko 1911	1

BARS
| Action Folie | 7 |
| Cocoon | 6 |

ACCOMMODATION
| Acropole | A |

0   50 m

when the so-called Long Walls, scattered remnants of which can still be seen, were built to connect it to the city. Today it's a substantial metropolis in its own right. The port, whose island ferries are the reason most people come here, has a gritty fascination of its own, typified

by the huge Sunday-morning **flea market**, concentrated around Odhós Skylítsi parallel to the rail tracks behind the metro station. The real attractions of the place, though, are around the small-boat harbours of **Zéa Marina** and **Mikrolímano** on the opposite side of the peninsula. Here, the upscale residential areas are alive with attractive waterfront cafés, bars and restaurants, and there's an excellent archeological museum. Above all, Athenians come to Pireás to eat on the waterfront, and the excellent fish tavernas are extremely busy at weekends.

Pireás Archeological Museum

Hariláou Trikoúpi 31 ☏ 210 45 21 598. Tues–Sun 8.30am–3pm. €3.
An excellent little museum,

many of whose displays were dragged from the harbour bed. Specially good are the second-century-AD stone reliefs of battles between Greeks and Amazons, apparently mass-produced for export to Rome, and a huge grave monument that's more like a miniature temple. The star of the show, however, must be the bronze *kouros* (idealized male statue) of Apollo; dating from 530–520 BC, this is the earliest known life-size bronze.

Athens' beaches and coastal transport

People swim from the rocks or sea wall almost anywhere on the coast southeast of Pireás – especially the older generation (the youth tend to head down towards the fleshpots and pay beaches of Glyfádha) – but the closest pleasant beach to the centre is Edem, reached by tram to the Edem or Váthis stops. A small patch of sand with cafés and tavernas, this is busy and urban but fine for a quick swim and sunbathe, and, remarkably, has Blue Flag status. There are other small, free beaches near the Váthis and Flisvós tram stops. Almost all of the really good beaches within easy reach of Athens, however, demand payment for entry. For your money you'll get clean sand, lifeguards, somewhere to buy food and drink, a lounger (usually at extra cost) and a variety of other facilities including beach volleyball, massage, fun parks and all sorts of water sports. Some of the fanciest, in Glyfádha and Vouliagméni, charge upwards of €10 per person at weekends (the *Astir Palace* hotel charges an exorbitant €45); more basic places cost €3–5. There are plenty of places to swim for free, but this may mean from the rocks, or a long hike from the road. The best sandy beach with free access is at Skhiniás (p.147), but that's a long way out on the northeast Attic coast. On summer weekends, every beach – and the roads to them – will be packed.

Among the better pay-beaches are Áyios Kósmas (summer daily 9am–8.30pm; €5, children €2), a relatively quiet choice at Ag. Kosmas 2 tram stop; Asteria (summer daily 8am–8pm; €5, €10 weekends, children half-price), a slightly glam and busy choice right in the heart of Glyfádha; Voúla A & B (summer daily 7am–9pm; €4), large twin beaches in Voúla between Glyfádha and Vouliagméni, cheap and cheerful with decent facilities; and Vouliagméni A (summer daily 8am–8pm; €5), on the main road in Vouliagméni, with few facilities but a lovely setting.

As far as Glyfádha the easiest transport option is the tram, and at most stops you'll be able to find somewhere to swim. For the better beaches beyond Glyfádha, though, you'll have to transfer to the bus. The main routes from Central Athens to Glyfádha are the #A2 or #E2 express (which go as far as Voúla), #A3 or #B3, all of which leave from Akadhimías. The #A1 or #E1 run from Pireás all the way along the coast to Voúla. For beaches further out, transfer onto local services #114 (Glyfádha–Kavoúri–Vouliagméni) or #115/6 (Glyfádha–Vouliagméni–Várkiza). If you drive, be warned that parking is a nightmare, especially in Glyfádha and Vouliagméni; the pay beaches all have parking, though some charge extra.

▲ PAY BEACH, VOÚLA

Glyfádha and around

Athens' southern suburbs form an almost unbroken line along the coast all the way from Pireás to Vouliagméni, some 20km away. This is the city's summer playground and the centre of it – for shopping, clubbing, dining or posing on the beach – is **Glyfádha**, a bizarre mix of glitz and suburbia. At weekends, half of Athens seems to decamp down here. The epicentre is around the crescent of Leofóros Angélou Metáxa, lined with shops and malls, with the tram running down the centre and streets of cafés and restaurants heading off on either side. Glyfádha merges almost indistinguishably into its neighbour Voúla, and then into quieter, more upmarket **Kavoúri** and **Vouliagméni**. The latter is one of the city's posher suburbs, and its beautiful cove beaches are a traditional hangout of Athens' rich and famous. Last stop for the local buses is Várkiza, more of a seaside resort pure and simple.

If you are prepared to walk a bit, or are driving and happy to battle the locals for parking space, then some of the best beaches can be found around the **Vouliagméni peninsula**, off the main road. Immediately after Voúla B pay beach, a road turns off to Kavoúri, past the *Divani Palace Hotel* and some packed free beaches with excellent tavernas. Further along on this Kavoúri side of the peninsula are some still better, less crowded, free beaches: the #114 bus runs a little way inland, not far from these. Carrying on round, you get to Vouliagméni itself, with beautiful little coves, a few of which remain free, and eventually rejoin the main road by Vouliagméni A beach. Beyond Vouliagméni the road runs high above the coast en route to Várkiza; the rocky shore a steep climb below, known as **Limanákia**, is largely nudist and has a large gay attendance.

Kessarianí

Monastery ☎ 210 72 36 619.
Tues–Sun 8.30am–2.30pm. €2.50.
East of the centre on the lower slopes of Mount Imittós, **Kessarianí** grew up after the 1922 exchange of populations, thrown together by refugees who'd left everything behind in Turkey. You can still see traces of that history in some of the ramshackle streets and tiny houses around you, but these days it's a prosperous place, enjoying its fine position high above the central pollution yet only 5km out. There are some excellent tavernas here too.

The real reason to come, though, is **Kessarianí monastery**, some thirty to forty minutes' walk beyond the houses, on a path that follows the main road. Here you're starting to climb the mountain and, despite the proximity of the new Imittós ring road, it is extraordinarily peaceful. The sources of the River Ilissos provide for extensive gardens hereabouts, as they have since ancient times: Athenians still come to collect water from the local fountains, though these days you're strongly advised not to drink it. The monastery buildings date from the eleventh century, though the frescoes in the chapel (a classic, cross-in-square design) are much later – executed during the sixteenth and seventeenth centuries. It's a small place, and doesn't take long to see; don't miss the ram's head spouting spring water at the back of the church.

The monastery gardens and the pine-forested slopes round about are popular **picnic** and **hiking** spots for Athenians. Follow the paths above the monastery and you'll find a number of chapels and ruined buildings, many of them signposted. From the top – follow signs to Lófos Taxiarchoú – there are wonderful **views** across Athens to Pireás and the sea beyond, with the Acropolis in the foreground. To the north are the uniform blocks of Panepistimioúpoli, the university campus.

Kifissiá

Set on the leafy lower slopes of Mount Pendéli, about 10km north of the city centre at the end of Metro Line 1, **Kifissiá** is one of Athens' swishest

> **Kessarianí transport**
>
> Take blue bus #223 or #224 from Akadhimías to the terminus by Kessarianí municipal stadium, and then walk straight on for the monastery.

suburbs. In the nineteenth century the area began to develop as a bourgeois summer residence, cooler and healthier than the city centre. The original villas – Neoclassical, Swiss or simply vulgar – still hold their own amid the newer concrete models. The metro and downtown pollution helped accelerate development, but Kifissiá is still distinctly "old money", despite the fact that these days it has a thoroughly suburban atmosphere, and the local branches of Gucci and Chanel are housed in upmarket malls.

Still, it's a fascinating place to see how the other half lives, full of pricey cafés and bars where young locals preen themselves and chat on their mobiles. Shopping

▼ KESSARIANÍ

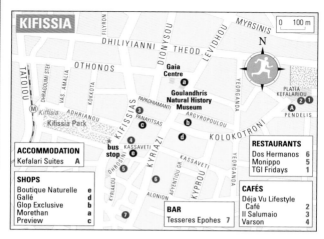

KIFISSIA

Gaia Centre **a**

Goulandhrís Natural History Museum **a**

0   100 m   N

ACCOMMODATION
Kefalari Suites   A

SHOPS
Boutique Naturelle   e
Gallé   d
Glop Exclusive   b
Morethan   a
Preview   c

bus stop

RESTAURANTS
Dos Hermanos   6
Monippo   5
TGI Fridays   1

CAFÉS
Déja Vu Lifestyle Café   2
Il Salumaio   3
Varson   4

BAR
Tesseres Epohes   7

and drinking aside, the **Goulandhrís Natural History Museum** (Mon–Sat 9am–2.30pm, Sun 10am–2.30pm; €5), at Levídhou 13, offers a more cultural excuse to visit. Set in a fine old mansion, the collection has especially good coverage of Greek birds, butterflies, and endangered species like the monk seal and loggerhead sea-turtle, plus a 250,000-specimen herbarium. Perhaps more interesting, especially for kids, the **Gaia Centre** (same hours; €5), part of the same complex but with its own entrance round the corner at Óthonos 100, offers a mildly interactive trip through the natural cycle of the earth and ecological issues. Labelling is in Greek only, but audio guides are available in English.

Cape Soúnio

Aktí Souníou – Cape Soúnio – on the southern tip of Attica some 70km from the city centre, is one of the most imposing spots in Greece, for centuries a landmark for boats sailing between Pireás and the islands and an equally dramatic vantage-point from which to look out over the Aegean. On its tip stands the captivating fifth-century-BC **Temple of Poseidon** (daily 9.30am–sunset; €5), built in the time of Pericles as part of a major sanctuary to the sea god and now in a picturesque state of semi-ruin.

The temple owes much of its fame to Lord Byron, who visited in 1810, carved his name on the nearest pillar (an unfortunate and much-copied

Kifissiá transport

Kifissiá is the northernmost stop on the metro, 35 minutes or so from Omónia, passing the Olympic site at Iríni along the way. There are also numerous buses, including the #550, which heads through the centre via Syngroú and Vasilíssis Sofías, and the #E7, #A7 and #B7, all of which start from Platía Káningos near Omónia.

precedent) and immortalized the place in verse:

Place me on Sunium's marbled steep,

Where nothing, save the waves and I,

May hear our mutual murmurs sweep;

There, swan-like, let me sing and die:

A land of slaves shall ne'er be mine –

Dash down yon cup of Samian wine!

from Don Juan

In summer, at least, there is faint hope of silent solitude, unless you slip into the site before the tour groups arrive or after they've left. Despite this, the setting is still wonderful – on a clear day, the view takes in the islands of Kéa, Kýthnos and Sérifos to the southeast, Égina and the Peloponnese to the west – and the temple as evocative a ruin as any in Greece. Doric in style, it was probably built by the architect of the Hephaisteion in the Athens Agora.

The rest of the site is of more academic interest. There are remains of a fortification wall around the sanctuary; a *propylaion* (entrance hall) and *stoa*; cuttings for two shipsheds; and the foundations of a small Temple of Athena.

Below the promontory are several tavernas at the far end. The port of Lávrio, a little further round the coast, has numerous cafés and restaurants, as well as a one-room **Archeological Museum** (Tues–Sun 9am–3pm; €2) with finds from the site.

Rafína

The east coast is a favourite weekend and holiday escape for jaded Athenians, many of whom have second homes out here. The main route out of the city leads straight for the little port of **Rafína**, from where you can head off to numerous islands, including nearby Évvia. Boats aside, the appeal of the place is mainly gastronomic: overlooking the harbour is a line of excellent seafood restaurants, many with roof terraces and a ringside view of the comings and goings of the port. The pedestrianized square above the harbour is also a lively place, ringed with cafés and rather cheaper eating options.

Marathon

The site of the **battle of Marathon**, the most famous and arguably most important military victory in Athenian history, is not far from the village of **Marathónas**, 42km from Athens. Here, in 490 BC, a force of 9000 Athenians and

▼ TEMPLE OF POSEIDON AT CAPE SOÚNIO

Soúnio transport

Orange KTEL Attikis buses leave Athens from the terminal on Mavrommatéon at the southwest corner of the Pedhíon Áreos Park. For Soúnio via the coast (€4.60; roughly 2hr) they depart every hour on the half-hour from 6.30am to 5.30pm; there's also a more central (but in summer, very full) stop ten minutes later on Filel-línon, south of Sýndagma (corner of Xenofóndos). Returns are hourly from 9.30am to 7.30pm, plus a couple of extra early-morning departures and a final one at 8pm. On the less-attractive inland route to Lávrio and Soúnio there are half-hourly departures from 5.45am to 6.45pm, not as frequently to Lávrio from then until 10.30pm (only a few of these continue to Soúnio). Drivers can take either route or complete a circuit, but there's little to see in the interior, where the road takes you via the airport and the toll motorway; and unless you're based in the northern suburbs it will probably be slower.

1000 of their Plataian allies defeated a Persian army 25,000 strong. After the victory a runner was sent to Athens to declare the news: having run the first marathon, he delivered his message and dropped dead. Just 192 Athenians died in the battle (compared to some 6000 Persians), and the burial mound where they were laid, the **Týmfos Marathóna** (Tues–Sun 8.30am–3pm; €3),

▼ FERRY, RAFÍNA

can still be seen, off the main road between Rafína and Marathónas. It is a quietly impressive monument, though surrounded now by one-way roads installed for the Olympic marathon race, which followed the route of the original marathon, over the hills from here to central Athens. The **Mound of the Plataians**, where the eleven Plataians (including a 10-year-old boy) who died were laid to rest, is about 5km away, near the edge of the mountain; there's also an **archeological museum** (Tues–Sun 8.30am–3pm; €3) here, with a sparse collection of artefacts mainly from the local Cave of Pan, a deity believed to have aided the victory.

Marathónas village itself is a dull place, though plentifully endowed with cafés and restaurants for the passing trade, and with now-neglected Olympic facilities (the rowing lake was also nearby).

Paralía Marathónas and Skhiniás

The coast around Marathon has some great stretches of sand. **Áyios Pandelímonas**, also known as Paralía Marathónas, is straight on past the burial

East-coast transport

There are buses to Rafína (40min) and to Marathónas (many via the beaches at Skhiniás) half-hourly throughout the day from the KTEL Attikis terminal on Mavrommatéon at the southwest corner of the Pedhíon Áreos Park. Ramnous is not realistically accessible by public transport. The main route for drivers is straight out on Messoyíon (following airport signs) onto the eastbound Leofóros Marathónos, which heads straight for Rafína and Marathon.

mound. There's only a small beach here, but a string of excellent waterfront fish-tavernas and an open-air movie theatre ensure plenty of local visitors in summer.

There's a far better beach to the north at **Skhiniás**, a long, pine-backed strand with shallow water, big enough to allow some chance of escaping the crowds. Marathon buses run along the road behind the beach, where there are a number of stops. At the southern end are a number of cordoned-off pay-beach sections offering cafés, showers, loungers and water sports; the central section of the beach, beyond the Olympic rowing and kayaking centre, is the least developed, with numerous tracks leading through the pines from the road to the sand. At the northern end there's some low-key development, mainly in the form of cafés and scattered tavernas on the sand. Towards Rafína, the coast around **Néa Mákri** is much more developed.

Ramnous

Summer daily 8am–5.30pm; winter Tues–Sun 8.30am–3pm. €2. The little-visited ruins of Ramnous occupy an isolated, atmospheric site above the sea, with magnificent views across the strait to Évvia. The site was an Athenian lookout point from the earliest times,

and remains of walls and fortifications can clearly be seen continuing way below the fenced site, all the way down to the rocky shore.

Within the site, the principal ruin is a Doric **Temple of Nemesis**, goddess of divine retribution. Pausanias records that the Persians incurred her wrath by their presumption in bringing with them to Greece a giant marble block upon which they intended to commemorate their victory. They met their nemesis, however, at the battle of Marathon, and the Athenians used the marble to create a statue instead. There are also the remains of a smaller temple dedicated to Themis, goddess of justice, and a section of ancient road.

Eleusis (Elefsína)

Tues–Sun 8am–7pm. €3. The **Sanctuary of Demeter** at Eleusis, on the edge of the modern town of Elefsína, was one of the most important in the ancient Greek world. For two millennia, the ritual ceremonies known as the Mysteries (see box, below) were performed here. Today, the extensive **ruins** of the sanctuary occupy a low hill on the coast right in the heart of modern Elefsína's industrial blight. The site offers something of an escape from its surroundings: from outside the museum, at one of the highest

▲ RAMNOUS

points, the gulf and its rusty shipping even manage to look attractive.

The best plan on arrival is to head straight for the **museum**, which features models of the sanctuary at various stages in its history: Eleusis is impressively large, with huge walls and gates some of which date back to Mycenaean times, but the numerous eras of building can also be confusing, especially as signage is poor and mainly in Greek. As well as the models and maps, the museum has some excellent finds from the site, especially Roman statuary (though also some much older objects). Exploring outside, the most important structure of ancient Eleusis was the

The Mysteries of Eleusis

The ancient Mysteries had an effect on their initiates that was easily the equal of any modern cult. According to Pindar, who experienced the rites in Classical times and, like all others, was bound on pain of death not to reveal their content, anyone who has "seen the holy things [at Eleusis] and goes in death beneath the earth is happy, for he knows life's end and he knows the new divine beginning".

Established in Mycenaean times, perhaps as early as 1500 BC, the cult centred around the figure of Demeter, the goddess of corn, and the myth of her daughter Persephone's annual descent into and resurrection from the underworld, which came to symbolize the rebirth of the crops and the miracle of fertility. By the fifth century BC the cult had developed into a sophisticated annual festival, attracting up to 30,000 people every autumn from all over the Greek world. The ceremonies lasted nine days: the Sacred Objects (identity unknown, but probably sheaves of fungus-infected grain, or vessels containing the magic potion) were taken to Athens, where they were stored in the Ancient Agora for four days. Various rituals took place in the city, many on the Acropolis but also mass bathing and purification in the sea at Fáliro. Finally a vast procession brought the objects back, following the Sacred Way to the sanctuary at Eleusis. Here over the final days initiates took part in the final rituals of *legomena* (things said), *dhromena* (things done) and *dheiknumena* (things shown). One theory suggests that these rituals involved drinking a potion containing grain-ergot fungus, producing similar effects to those of modern psychedelic drugs. The Mysteries survived well into the Christian era, but eventually fell victim to the new orthodoxy.

Demeter is said to have threatened to render the land permanently barren if her worship at Eleusis ever ceased. Looking at the ecological havoc wreaked by the area's industry, it would seem that the curse has been fulfilled.

Eleusis transport

City buses #A16, #B16 or express #E16 head from Platía Eleftherías (aka Platía Koumoundhoúrou), on Pireós in central Athens, to Elefsína. Between them they run several times an hour every day. In Elefsína the buses head straight down the main street, Ierá Odhós: get off where you see the sign, and the sanctuary is a short walk down towards the sea. This is also the route to drive, ignoring confusing signs on the outskirts of Elefsína.

Telesterion. This windowless Hall of Initiation lay at the heart of the cult, and it was here that the priests of Demeter would exhibit the **Sacred Objects** and speak "the Unutterable Words".

Shops

Boom
Platía Katráki 1, Glyfádha. Right on the main square at the entrance to Glyfádha, a large fashion store on three huge floors with a coffee lounge.

Boutique Naturelle
Kassavéti 4, Kifissiá. Handmade cosmetics and soaps at competitive prices.

BSB
Fívos 12, cnr, Angélou Metáxa, Glyfádha. Greek fashion-label that makes an interesting alternative clothes to the well-known names all around.

Celestino
Angélou Metáxa 15–17, Glyfádha. Local designer worth checking out for unusual attire.

Gallé
Kolokotróni 10, Kifissiá. Fashion store with clothing, accessories and shoes from the likes of Paul Smith and Givenchy as well as local designers. Marginally easier on the wallet than neighbours like Gucci and Kenzo.

Gallery Biz Art
Ziríni 10, Kifissiá. Fine Art-Deco ornaments and sculptures and a large range of oil paintings; a little way from the centre but well worth a browse.

Glou Exclusive
Koloktróni 9, Kifissiá. In the very heart of the Kifissiá shopping area, this Greek men's-fashion chain is reasonably priced, though the *Exclusive* bit of the name indicates that it's only the upper end of their range on offer here.

Lak
Angélou Metáxa 24–26, Glyfádha. Designer clothes for well-heeled and super-trendy youngsters.

▲ ELEUSIS

▲ SHOPPING AT KIFISSIÁ

Morethan

Levídhou 11, Kifissiá. Functional designer objects for the home. Interesting, quirky and portable.

Nike exclusivesports

Angélou Metáxa 32, Glyfádha. Large selection of Nike sports goods.

Preview

Panayítsas 6, Kifissiá. Designer footwear – good range of lesser-known brands, though still expensive.

Tommy Hilfiger

Angélou Metáxa 14, Glyfádha. The definitive Glyfádha label.

Cafés

Déja Vu Lifestyle Café

Platía Kefalaríou, Kifissiá. The name says it all – come here to see and be seen while lingering over your *cappuccino freddo* or salad lunch.

Ego Mio

Zissimopoúlo 10, Glyfádha. One of a crowd of glam, upmarket café-bars on this street just off the main shopping drag in the heart of Glyfádha.

Pagoto Manía

Konstantinoupoléos 5, Glyfádha. Wonderful ice cream in a huge variety of flavours, plus all the usual café fare.

Il Salumaio

Panayítsas 3, cnr Kifissías, Kifissiá. Marvellous, expensive delicatessen with a few tables inside and out. Great food, but really worth it for the pure Kifissiá ambience – elegant, snobbish and glam.

Varson

Kassavéti 5, Kifissiá. This huge, old-fashioned café/patisserie is an Athens institution. Home-made yogurts, jams and sticky cakes to take away or to enjoy with a coffee in the cavernous interior or in a quiet courtyard out back.

Restaurants

Akhinós

Aktí Themistokléous 51, Pireás ☎210 45 26 944. Wonderful seafood and traditional Greek specialities served on a covered terrace overlooking a small beach just round the corner from the Naval Museum. Pricey if you go for the fish, but less so than harbourfront alternatives. Book at weekends.

Akriogiali

Soúnio beach, by the Aegeon hotel ☎229 20 39 107. Oct–April closed eves. Simple beachside taverna with both character and history – a number of illustrious Greek guests have dined here. The food, mainly fish, is simple but cooked to perfection.

Akti

Possidhónos 6, Vouliagméni ☎210 89 60 448. On the main road just beyond the Vouliagméni peninsula, with waterfront tables and great views, this is a top-class fish taverna. Fish is expensive and so is Vouliagméni; by those standards €50–60 for a fish or lobster main-course is reasonable value. Waterfront tables are very heavily in demand; booking is essential.

Attos

Aktí Koumoundhoúrou 44, Mikrolímano, Pireás ☎210 41 34 998. In contrast to the high-luxe places surrounding it, *Attos* goes for an island feel, with hand-painted tables and beach scenes. Still mainly fish, but a wide variety of *mezes*, and slightly lower prices and a younger crowd than its neighbours.

Buffalo Bill's

Kýprou 13, Glyfádha ☎210 89 43 128. Eves only, plus Sun lunchtime. Get into the Glyfádha mood at this lively, atmospheric Tex-Mex joint. As you'd expect, there are tacos, steaks and chilli on offer, plus margaritas by the jugful.

Dos Hermanos

Kyriazí 24, Kifissiá ☎210 80 87 906. Closed Mon. Decent Mexican food – tacos, burritos, fajitas – and tasty margaritas in a lively, late-opening bar-restaurant.

PLACES Around Athens

▼ LUNCH AT ATTOS

PLACES

Around Athens

George's Steak House

Konstantinoupóleos 4, Glyfádha ☎210 894 6020. Despite the name this is a fairly traditional Greek grill-house, large, reasonably priced and very popular. Located on a side-street crowded with restaurants close to the main Platía Katráki tram stop. Excellent lamb chops and meatballs.

Island

Limanákia Vouliagménis, 27km on Athens–Soúnio road between Vouliagméni and Várkiza ☎210 96 53 563. Summer eves only, 9.30pm till late (club from 11pm). Beautiful bar/restaurant/club with a breathtaking clifftop setting which, as the name suggests, evokes island life; very chic and not as expensive as you might expect at €15–25 for a main course. Modern Mediterranean food and tapas lounge. You'll need to book.

Jimmy and the Fish

Aktí Koumoundhoúrou 46, Mikrolímano, Pireás ☎210 41 24 417. Excellent, glamorous and inevitably expensive fish-taverna occupying the prime position among the harbourside places on

Mikrolímano. Booking is essential at weekends.

Ta Kavoúria tou Asimáki

Limáni, Rafína ☎229 40 24 551. The first of the harbourside tavernas as you walk down from town, and arguably the best, with a fine view from its rooftop tables. Fish is the inevitable speciality, but plenty of other choice too.

Masa

Ethnikís Andístasis 240, Kessarianí ☎210 72 36 177. Closed Mon. Straightforward, inexpensive Greek taverna with good, simple food and barrel wines.

Monippo

Dhrosíni 12, Kifissiá ☎210 62 31 440. Wide range of *mezédhes* from all over Greece and smart, modern decor make this a typical Kifissiá hangout. It's better value than most, though, and often has music on Friday and Saturday nights.

Ouzeri Limeni

Platía Plastíra 17, Rafína ☎229 40 24 750. One of many choices on the pedestrianized square above the harbour, *Limeni* serves excellent, inexpensive *mezes*.

▼ MIKROLÍMANO

▲ WATERFRONT TAVERNA AT RAFINA

Syrtaki

Near Soúnio, on road towards Lávrio ☎ 229 20 39 125. Popular place with a wide range of standard taverna fare, including seafood at reasonable prices.

TGI Fridays

Koloktróni 35, Platía Kefalaríou, Kifissiá ☎ 210 62 33 947. Archetypal Kifissiá: burgers, ribs and mobile phones all round, but considerably classier than the average branch of this chain.

Time

Skouzé 14, Pireás ☎ 210 42 85 937. The cosmopolitan nature of Pireás is very much in evidence here: this authentic, inexpensive Indo-Pakistani restaurant caters largely to locals, in the midst of a small ethnic and red-light quarter.

Trata

Platía Anayeníseos 7–9, Kessarianí ☎ 210 72 91 533. Closed Aug. Well-known fish restaurant on a square with several tavernas just off the main Ethnikís Andístasis. Fish is always pricey in Athens, but this is good value.

Tria Adhelfia

Paralía Marathónas, 300m north of the village centre ☎ 229 40 56 461.

Simple seafood taverna with a stunning waterfront position.

Vincenzo

Yiannitsopoúlou 1, Platía Espéridhon, Glyfádha ☎ 210 89 41 310. Good, reasonably priced Italian fare, including excellent pizzas from a wood oven.

To Voliótiko 1911

Goúnari 9, Pireás ☎ 210 42 25 905. Traditional Greek taverna right in the heart of the port area. Gastronomy isn't this area's forte, but this is good value, and a good option if you're waiting for a ferry.

Bars

Action Folie

Aktí Dhilavéri 9–11, Mikrolímano, Pireás ☎ 210 41 74 325. Café-bar that's open all day and most of the night, every day. The tables outside make a good place to check out all the action of this buzzing nightlife area.

Cocoon

Aktí Koumoundoúrou, Mikrolímano, Pireás. There are dozens of bars and cafés around Mikrolímano in Pireás and along the coast to the east, towards SEF. *Cocoon* is one of the biggest, with three

▲ TAVERNA AT LÁVRIO

floors as well as a waterside enclosure and an ambience that ranges from waterfront lounging over coffee by day to early-hours clubbing.

Tesseres Epohes

Platía Ayíou Dhimítriou 13, Kifissiá ☎210 80 18 233. The "Four Seasons" is an attractive bar-*mezedhopolío* where you can enjoy *mezédhes*, drinks, snacks and, on Thursday to Saturday evenings, excellent, unamplified live Greek music.

Clubs

Balux

Possidhónos 58, Glyfádha ☎210 89 41 620. Summer only. On Astéras beach in the heart of Glyfádha, *Balux* attracts a hip, moneyed, young crowd. The music may be anything from hip-hop to 80s disco.

Envy

Paralía Ayíou Kosmá, right by Áyios Kósmas beach ☎210 98 52 994. Summer only. Huge complex right on the shore with café, restaurant and palm trees to complement the party-atmosphere club. Regular sunset parties, Greek nights and the like make this typical of the slicker summer-only beach clubs.

Island

Limanákia Vouliagménis, km 27 on Athens–Soúnio road between Vouliagméni and Várkiza ☎210 96 53 563. Summer only. Stunning clifftop setting attracts a chic, stylish crowd. One way to be sure of making it past the queue and the bouncers is to book into the restaurant (see p.152).

Venue

Km 30 on the Athens–Soúnio road, Várkiza ☎210 89 70 333. Summer only. *Venue*'s lush setting and eclectic selection of dance music – including some Greek – entice a young crowd.

Further afield

With the use of a hire car or by taking one of many tours available out of Athens, you can visit a wealth of sites and attractions, all within a few hours' reach. Highlights include the stunning ruins of Delphi (site of the famous Delphic Oracle in ancient times), mountain hiking on the slopes of Mount Parnassós and the impressive ancient sites of Tiryns and Mycenae. From the port of Pireás, too, you can easily jump on a comfortable ferry or fast hydrofoil and be on a Greek island in the Argo-Saronic gulf within an hour or two, making for some wonderfully varied day-trips – although you may want to enjoy longer outings by taking advantage of the countless places to stay you'll find everywhere you go.

Delphi

Sacred Precinct daily: summer 8.30am–6.45pm; winter 8am–5pm. Museum daily: summer 8am–6.45pm; winter 8.30am–2.45pm. €9 joint ticket.

Perched on the slopes of a high mountain terrace and dwarfed to either side by the massive crags of Mount Parnassós, it's easy to see why the ancients believed Delphi to be the centre of the earth. As if the natural setting and occasional earthquake and avalanche weren't enough to confirm a divine presence, this, according to Plutarch, was where a rock chasm was discovered that exuded strange vapours and reduced people to frenzied, incoherent and prophetic mutterings. Thus was born the famous **Delphic Oracle**, to which kings and simple citizens flocked in an attempt to foresee the future.

Delphi is a large and complex ruin, best taken in two stages, with the sanctuary and precinct ideally at the beginning or end of the day, or (in winter) at lunchtime, to escape the crowds.

The **Sacred Precinct** contains most of the sights – including the Temple of Apollo, the impressive theatre and the stadium. The Marmaria, or **Sanctuary of Athena**, lies further east, about a ten-minute walk along the main road and on the opposite side. The most conspicuous building in the precinct is the **Tholos**, a fourth-century-BC rotunda. Three of its dome-columns

▲ THOLOS, DELPHI

and their entablature have been reconstructed but, while these amply demonstrate the original beauty of the building, its ultimate purpose still remains a mystery. The historic **Castalian spring** is located on a sharp bend between the Marmaria and the Sacred Precinct. It is marked by niches for votive offerings and by the remains of an archaic fountain-house – water still flows from a cleft in the Phaedriades cliffs.

Modern Dhelfí, just west of the site, is almost entirely geared to tourism with easy access not just to the ancient site but also the popular skiing centre of Mount Parnassós. There is a helpful tourist office (Mon–Fri 8am–2.30pm; ☎226 50 82 900) in the town hall.

If you don't want an organized tour, up to six **buses** a day run direct to Delphi from Athens, leaving from the Liossíon terminal. Drivers should take the old road towards Thebes.

Aráhova

The strung-out village of Aráhova, dwarfed by the peaks of Parnassós, is a picturesque little place, with its vernacular architecture, stone walls, wooden eaves, and shops selling all kinds of craftware and foodstuffs. During the winter it's popular with skiers, but it's worth a brief stop at any time of year to browse the wide variety of local produce – including wine, cheese and local pasta known as *hilópittes* – and to wander the attractive backstreets winding

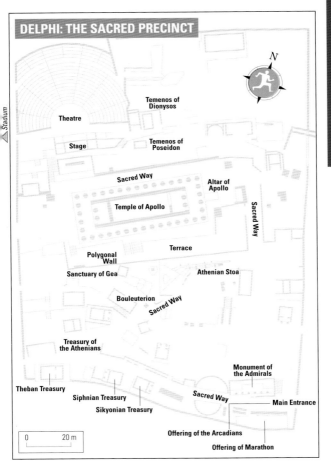

DELPHI: THE SACRED PRECINCT

- Stadium
- Theatre
- Stage
- Temenos of Dionysos
- Temenos of Poseidon
- Sacred Way
- Altar of Apollo
- Temple of Apollo
- Sacred Way
- Terrace
- Polygonal Wall
- Sanctuary of Gea
- Athenian Stoa
- Bouleuterion
- Sacred Way
- Treasury of the Athenians
- Monument of the Admirals
- Theban Treasury
- Siphnian Treasury
- Sikyonian Treasury
- Sacred Way
- Main Entrance
- Offering of the Arcadians
- Offering of Marathon

0   20 m

off the busy main road. There's a wide selection of good places to wine and dine, many distinctly upmarket; not all are open in summer, however.

The local festival of Áyios Yeóryios (April 23, or the Tuesday after Easter if this date falls within Lent), centred on the church at the top of the hill, is the excuse for almost two days of continuous partying, and one of the best opportunities in the region to see authentic folk-dancing.

There are daily buses to and from Athens and Delphi.

Mount Parnassós

Mount Parnassós, rising to almost 2500 metres at its highest point, is a popular climbing and walking destination, as well as a ski centre in winter. The heights are easily accessible, and though they no longer rank as complete

The Delphic Oracle

The origins of the Delphic Oracle are uncertain but it was believed by the ancients that the first oracle established on this spot was dedicated to Gea (Mother Earth) and to Poseidon (the Earth Shaker). Subsequently the serpent Python, son of Gea, was installed in a nearby cave, and communication made through the Pythian priestess. Python was later slain by Apollo, whose cult had been imported from Crete. Legend has it that he arrived in the form of a dolphin – hence the name Delphoi.

For over a thousand years thereafter, a steady stream of pilgrims made its way up the dangerous mountain paths to Delphi in order to seek divine direction in matters of war, worship, love or business. On arrival they would sacrifice a sheep or a goat and, depending on the omens, wait to submit questions inscribed on lead tablets. The Pythian priestess, a simple and devout village woman of fifty or more years in age, would chant her prophecies from a tripod positioned over the oracular chasm.

Many of the oracular answers were equivocal. Croesus, for example, was told that if he embarked on war against neighbouring Persia he would destroy a mighty empire; he did – his own. But it's hard to imagine that the oracle would have retained its popularity and influence for so long without offering predominantly sound advice.

One theory suggests that the prophetic inspiration of the Oracle was due to geologic phenomena. The oracle may have been deliberately sited over a geological or earthquake fault line that emitted trance-inducing gases such as methane or ethane, which could have produced the kind of trances and behaviour described by ancient witnesses of the Pythian priestesses.

wilderness, thanks to the ski station above Aráhova and its accompanying paraphernalia of lifts, snack bars and access roads, the area remains an attractive break from the city.

The best routes for walkers are those up from Dhelfí to the Corycian cave (practicable April–Nov, but not in midsummer without a dawn start), or the ascent to the summit of Mount Liákoura (2455m) that commences from the Yerondóvrakhos ski station (May–Oct only). With your own transport you could drive up the mountain from Aráhova on the south, or from Lílea, Polýdhrosos or Amfilia on the north slope, any of which can easily be combined with a walk.

▼ TEMPLE OF APOLLO

▲ CORINTH

Corinth

Corinth daily: summer 8.30am–7pm; winter 8am–5pm. €6. Acrocorinth: summer daily 8am–7pm; winter Tues–Sun 8.30am–3pm. Free. The ruins of ancient Corinth, which displaced Athens as capital of the Greek province in Roman times, occupy a rambling sequence of sites that encompass sections of ancient walls, outlying stadiums, gymnasiums and necropolises. The highlight here is the majestic ruin of the Temple of Apollo, a fifth-century-BC survivor of the Classical era. Still more compelling, though, are the ruins of the medieval city, which occupy the stunning acropolis of **Acrocorinth**, towering 565m above the ancient city on an enormous mass of rock, still largely encircled by two kilometres of wall. This became one of Greece's most powerful fortresses during the Middle Ages.

There's a four-kilometre climb to the entrance gate (an hour's walk, or taxis are usually available at ancient Corinth), but it's worth it: from the top, overlooking the Saronic and Corinthian gulfs, you really get a sense of the site's strategic importance. Amid the extensive remains, you wander through a jumble of chapels, mosques, houses and battlements, erected in turn by Greeks, Romans, Byzantines, Frankish crusaders, Venetians and Turks.

Epidauros

Site: summer daily 8am–7pm, winter 8am–5pm. Museum: same hours but opens noon on Mon. €6 joint ticket. Epidauros (Epídhavros) is visited primarily for its stunning ancient **theatre**, built around 330–320 BC, whose setting makes a compelling venue for productions of Classical drama as part of the annual Hellenic Festival (see p.35). With its backdrop of rolling hills, Epidauros's 14,000-seat theatre merges perfectly into the landscape – so well, in fact, that it was rediscovered only in the nineteenth century. Constructed with mathematical precision, it has near-perfect acoustics – such that you can hear coins, or even matches, dropped in the circular orchestra from the highest of the 54 tiers of seats.

The theatre, however, is just one component of what was one of the most important sanctuaries in the ancient world, dedicated to the healing god Asklepios. A place of pilgrimage for half a millennium, from the sixth century BC into Roman times,

▲ EPIDAUROS

it's now a World Heritage site. Close by the theatre is a small museum, which is best visited before you explore the rest of the sanctuary – most of the ruins visible today are just foundations, so dropping in here helps identify some of the former buildings. The finds displayed show the progression of medical skills and cures used at the **Asklepion**; there are tablets recording miraculous cures alongside advanced-looking surgical instruments.

Náfplio

A lively, beautifully sited town, Náfplio exudes a grand, slightly faded elegance, inherited

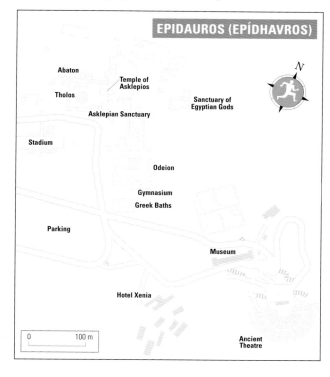

EPIDAUROS (EPÍDHAVROS)

N

Abaton

Temple of
Asklepios

Tholos

Sanctuary of
Egyptian Gods

Asklepian Sanctuary

Stadium

Odeion

Gymnasium

Greek Baths

Parking

Museum

Hotel Xenia

0   100 m

Ancient
Theatre

from the days when it was the fledgling capital of modern Greece in the early nineteenth century. The postcard-pretty old town, with its paved and mostly pedestrianized streets, has an abundance of colourful and tastefully decorated restaurants and handicraft shops, and there's a pleasant buzz that you don't often witness in Greek towns. For the fit, the climb up to the twin fortresses of **Palamídhi** (daily: summer 8am–7pm; winter 8am–6.30pm; €4), out on the headland and overlooking the old town, is well worth the effort. The town's third fort, the stunning Boúrtzi, occupies the Ayíou Theodhórou islet offshore from the harbour, and was built in 1473 by the Venetians to control the shipping lane to the town and to much of Árgos bay.

Café life – swelled at weekends by crowds of visiting Athenians – reaches the heights of urban chic in the well-patronized cafés lining the palm-tree-fringed western seafront of Bouboulínas. Things are quieter on Platía Syndágmatos, where places stay open late.

You can get to Náfplio by bus or – much slower but much more attractive – by the twice-daily train. Both bus and train stations are within a 500m walk of the old town precinct.

Tiryns

Daily: summer 8am–7pm; winter 8.30am–3pm. €3. In Mycenaean times the ancient fortress of Tiryns (Tíryntha) commanded the coastal approaches to Árgos and Mycenae. The Aegean shore, however, gradually receded, leaving this impressive structure stranded on a low hillock in today's plains, surrounded by citrus groves, alongside a large modern prison. The setting is less impressive than that of its showy neighbour Mycenae, which in part explains why this highly accessible, substantial site is relatively empty of visitors; the opportunity to wander about Homer's "wall-girt Tiryns" in near-solitude is worth taking. The site lies just to the east of the main Árgos–Náfplio road, and frequent local buses drop off and pick up passengers outside.

▼ TIRYNS

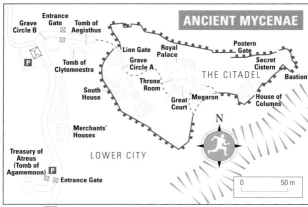

Modern village of Mykínes (2 km)

Mycenae

Daily: summer 8am–7.30pm; winter 8.3am–5pm. €8. Tucked into a fold of the hills just east of the road from Kórinthos to Árgos, the **citadel** at Mycenae (Mykínes) bears testament above all to the obsession of the German archeologist Heinrich Schliemann (who also excavated the site of Troy) with proving that the tales of Homer had their basis in fact.

The extensive site is made up of two parts – the citadel itself and the Treasury of Atreus. The most visually arresting part of the citadel is the Lion Gate, whose huge sloping gateposts

and walls were considered Cyclopean by later Greeks, who could only imagine that a Cyclops could have constructed them. Beyond the Lion Gate is an impressive Grave Circle known as "A" and originally thought by Schliemann to be the actual tomb of Agamemnon. It was here that the famous gold death-mask was found in 1876. The rest of the site is scattered over the hillside, while just down the road is the tremendously impressive **Treasury of Atreus**, which is what is now described as the **Tomb of Agamemnon**. This was certainly a royal burial vault

▼ MYCENAE

▲ FERRY TICKET BOOTHS

at a late stage in Mycenae's history, so the attribution to Agamemnon or his father is as good as any. Whoever it might have belonged to, this beehive-like structure is an impressive monument to Mycenaean building skills.

Égina

Barely an hour and a half from Pireás, the rural island of Égina can easily be visited in a day. Most visitors spend their day ambling around the boat-packed waterfront or through the backstreets of the island's main town – also called Égina. Making use of the decent local bus service, you could also head for the exceptionally well-preserved, beautiful fifth-century-BC **Temple of Afaia** (Tues–Sun 8am–5pm daily; €4), which stands in lonely vigil at the northeastern corner of the island; or the low-key fishing village of Pérdhika with its cosy harbour and fish tavernas that are often frequented by Athenian yachties; or perhaps the east-coast resort village of Ayía Marína.

There's a good selection of accommodation in the port of Égina, and plenty of tavernas – restaurants here tend to specialize in fish, usually rather cheaper than in Athens or Pireás. The island is also a big producer of pistachio nuts, and during the summer months you can see the orchards around the island laden with them.

Transport to and from the island is frequent and good; you've a choice of ferries or hydrofoils, and advance booking is unnecessary – just turn up at the ferry quay in Pireás and buy a ticket from the booths.

Angístri

Just one hour's ferry trip from Pireás – or fifteen minutes from Égina – Angístri is small enough to be explored on foot, from the port of Skála to the delightful little bay, beach and hamlet of Apónisos, with its two tiny offshore islets. On the way you'll pass Mýlos (Megalokhóri) and the small farming community of Limenária, set at the edge of a fertile plateau in the southeast corner of the island. There's a decent sandy beach at Skála, though you may find a little more seclusion at Halikádha pebble beach (clothing optional), backed by crumbling cliffs and pine-covered hills on the east side of the island.

Póros

Separated from the mainland by just a 450-metre strait, Póros (The Ford) is in fact

▲ PÓROS HARBOUR

two islands: Sferiá (occupied almost entirely by Póros Town), and the much more extensive Kalávria. Its proximity to Pireás means it's hugely popular, making Póros Town – which is exceptionally picturesque – a lively, animated place to be. The cafés, waterfront tavernas and restaurants entertain a seemingly endless flow of customers, while fishermen attempt to sell their catch to passers-by. There's little specific to seek out, although the hilltop clocktower and small, well-labelled **archeological museum** (Tues–Sun 8.30am–3pm; €2) are worth a look. For a more peaceful escape, head over to Kalávria, whose south coast is fringed by a succession of pine-shaded bays.

Ídhra

The port and town of Ídhra (Hydra), with tiers of greystone mansions and white-walled, red-tiled houses climbing steeply up from a perfect horseshoe harbour, make a magnificent spectacle. Both beautiful and peaceful – thanks to an almost total ban on motor vehicles – it is unsurprisingly popular. You'll see it at its best if you visit on a weekday or out of season: on

the plus side, the visitors mean plenty of excellent restaurants and cafés, getting less expensive as you head away from the waterfront.

The mansions themselves, most of them built during the eighteenth century on the accumulated wealth of a remarkable merchant fleet, were designed by Venetian and Genoese architects and are still the great monuments of the island. A town map is available if you are interested in seeking any out – some are labelled at the entrance with "*Oikía*" (home) and the family name.

Ídhra also reputedly has no fewer than 365 churches – a total claimed by many a Greek island, but here with some justice. The most important is the church of Panayía Mitropóleos, with a distinctive clocktower and a **Byzantine museum** (Tues–Sun 10am–5pm; €2). Thanks to the lack of transport, few people venture away from the town, so a short walk will take you to surprising isolation; there are no real sandy beaches, but numerous rocky coves are accessible (with less effort, you can also get to many by boat or water-taxi from the harbour).

Restaurants

Andonis

Pérdhika, 9km from Égina Town, Égina ☏ 229 70 61 443. The most popular of the fish tavernas on the harbour here. A little pricey, but the high-quality dishes are still good value.

Antica Gelateria di Roma

Farmakopoúlon 3 & Komnímou, just north of Platía Syndágmatos, Náfplio. Wonderful ice cream made on the premises from fresh fruit and local cream, in a delightfully old-fashioned setting. Also coffee and drinks.

Byzantio

Vassiléos Aléxandrou 15, Náfplio. Excellent, friendly taverna on a quiet corner of a beautiful street, with a varied menu and large portions.

Epikouros

Pavlou & Fredirikis 33, Dhelfí ☏ 226 50 83 250. One of the best eateries in Delphi, the wild-boar stew is particularly good here – and the view from the terrace is stunning.

Flisvos

Égina waterfront, by town beach, Égina. A lovely spot for simple, fresh grilled fish or meat; less pricey than most on the waterfront.

Gitoniko

Ídhra ☏ 229 80 53 615. About 500m inland from the port near Áyios Konstandínos church, this friendly taverna has great home-cooked specials (which run out early) plus grills and excellent fish. And a roof terrace too.

Kakanarakis

Vasilíssis Ólgas 18, Náfplio ☏ 275 20 25 371. Eves only. Lively place serving a variety of reasonably priced and dependably good *mezédhes*, plus dishes such as braised cockerel with noodles, and *kokkinistó* (meat simmered in tomato sauce).

Karavolos

Póros ☏ 229 80 26 158. Eves only. Busy taverna serving *karavólos* (snails) and other imaginative fare such as *saganáki* (small skillet) dishes. It's signposted from the western waterfront.

Kathestos

Póros harbour. On the seafront between the town hall and the museum, this is one of the best of the many seafood options.

Taverna Leonides

Epidauros ☏ 275 20 22 115. A friendly spot with a garden out back; book ahead if your visit coincides with a performance at the ancient theatre. Actors eat here after shows – photos on the wall testify to the patronage of Melina Mercouri, the Papandreous, François Mitterrand and Sir Peter Hall.

Mykinaiko

Mykínes, Mycenae ☏ 275 10 76 724. One of the best in the village in terms of both quality and value, with excellent oven-cooked dishes and a robust, draft red wine known as "Blood of Hercules" to wash it down.

Palia

Staïkopoúlou 6, Náfplio. Having served traditional, home-cooked oven dishes for almost 200 years, *Palia* is clearly getting something right.

Panagiota

Aráhova ☏ 226 70 32 735. A friendly, family-style taverna high above Aráhova, with fine, good-value lamb dishes, home-baked bread and rich chicken soup.

Parnassos

Metókhi, Angístri. It's worth the walk up the hill for the views and the good food here. Dine on *mayireftá* and enjoy the relaxing view down towards Skála.

Platanos

Póros ☎229 80 24 249. High up overlooking Póros port from a little square hosting a clutch of less obvious tavernas, *Platanos* specializes in meat dishes, and you can dine in the shade of a large plane-tree.

Steki

Ídhra Town. Just inland from the waterfront, with seating in a shady courtyard, *Steki* serves good-value home-cooked specials washed down with powerful local *retsina*.

Vakchos

Apóllonos 31, Dhelfí ☎226 50 83 250. One of the better-quality establishments in a village not particularly well known for great eateries. The view from this family place is quite stunning, and the food is good-quality traditional fare that's reasonable value for your euros.

Yeladhakis

Panayioti Irioti 28, behind the fish market, Égina ☎229 70 27 308. The best and least expensive of three rival seafood ouzerís here: you may have to wait for a table, but worth it for great octopus, sardines, shrimp and other fishy *mezédhes*.

Yiorgos

Skála, Angístri. A long-established, good-quality seafood taverna just above the jetty.

Accommodation

Hotels

Prices for accommodation are highly seasonal and, since the Olympics, well over half the city's hotels seemed to have been refurbished, raising their rates accordingly. The prices quoted in this guide represent the hotel's cheapest double room in high season; much of the year, you'll find rates are lower than this. By law, every room has to display its official rates on the back of the door: it is illegal for a hotelier to charge more than this, and you can normally expect to pay less. Most places have triple and even four-bed rooms, which can be a significant saving for a family or group.

Breakfast is included in the price at the more expensive hotels and is almost always available at extra cost if it's not included; check what you'll get, however, as the standard Greek hotel breakfast of a cup of weak coffee accompanied by a piece of dry cake and some jam is rarely worth paying for. Most of our recommendations will offer more than that – usually some form of buffet.

Pláka, Monastiráki, Makriyiánni and **Sýndagma** are all atmospheric neighbourhoods

within easy walking distance of the main sites; hotels here are also relatively expensive, however, and may be noisy. Formerly gritty and sleazy but rapidly being gentrified, Omónia's **bazaar area** is the city at its most colourful, while nearby **Thissío** is rather smarter and airier. **Koukáki**, slightly further out beyond Makriyiánni, has some good, quieter budget options. Most of the larger, modern hotels are on the busy avenues around Omónia, or further out.

Pláka

Acropolis House Kódhrou 6 ☎210 32 22 344, ✉htlacrhs@otenet.gr. Metro Sýndagma. A rambling, slightly dilapidated 150-year-old mansion much loved by its regulars – mostly students and academics. Furnishings are individual and some rooms have baths across the hall; not all are a/c, though most are naturally cool. Rates include use of fridge, shared books and other useful items left behind by previous guests. Discounts for longer stays. Rates include breakfast. €60.

Adonis Kódhrou 3 ☎210 32 49 737, ☎210 32 31 602. Metro Sýndagma. A 1960s low-rise *pension* across the street from *Acropolis House*, with some suites. Rather old-fashioned, but none the worse

---

Booking accommodation

Athens hotels and hostels can be packed to the gills in midsummer – August especially – but for most of the year you'll have no problem finding a bed. Having said that, many of the more popular hotels are busy all year round, so it makes sense to **book in advance**; almost every place listed here will have an English-speaking receptionist. If you do just set out and do the rounds, try to start as early as possible in the day. Once you locate a vacancy, ask to see the room before booking in – standards vary greatly even within the same building, and you can avoid occasional overcharging by checking the government-regulated room prices displayed by law on the back of the door in each room. Hotels throughout the city were refurbished for the Olympics, and some of these newly done-up places are very good value (at least by Athenian standards).

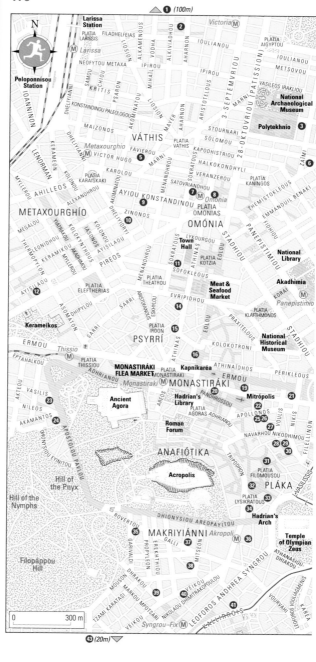

△ ❶ (100m)

N

Larissa
Station
PLATIA
LARISSIS
FILADHELFEIAS
Ⓜ Larissa
Peloponnísou
Station

PLATIA AIGYPTOU

Victoria Ⓜ

❷

IOULIANOU

METSOVOU

National
Archaeological
Museum

Polytekhnío ❸

VÁTHIS

❻

❺

OMÓNIA

Omonia Ⓜ ❽

❼

PLATIA
OMONIAS

❾

METAXOURGHÍO

❿

Town
Hall
PLATIA
KOTZIA

⓫

National
Library

Akadhimia

Panepistimio Ⓜ

Kerameikos

Meat &
Seafood
Market

⓬

⓮

PLATIA
IROON
⓯

National
Historical
Museum

MONASTIRÁKI
FLEA MARKET

PSYRRÍ

⓰

Kapnikaréa

Monastiraki Ⓜ MONASTIRÁKI

⓴

⓳

Mitrópolis ㉑

Ancient
Agora

Hadrian's
Library

PLATIA
AGORAS ADHRIANOU

㉒

㉕㉖

㉗

㉓

Roman
Forum

㉔

ANAFIÓTIKA

㉘㉙

㉚

Hill of
the Pnyx

Acropolis

㉛

PLATIA
FILOMOUSOU

㉜

PLÁKA

Hill of the
Nymphs

PLATIA
LYSIKRATOUS ㉝

㉞

Hadrian's
Arch

Filopáppou
Hill

㉟

MAKRIYIÁNNI

Akropoli Ⓜ ㊱

㊲

Temple
of Olympian
Zeus

㊳

㊴

㊵

Syngrou–Fix Ⓜ

㊶

0 ___ 300 m

㊸ (20m) ▽

HOSTELS & BACKPACKERS	
Hostel Aphrodite	1
Athens Backpackers	36
Athens International Youth Hostel	5
Athens Youth Hostel	42

HOTELS			
Acropolis House	28	Fresh Hotel	11
Acropolis View	35	Grande Bretagne	17
Adonis	29	Hermes	26
The Alassia	7	Herodion	37
Arethusa	21	Kouros	30
Art Gallery	39	Marble House	43
Athenian Callirhoe	41	Metropolis	19
Athens Studios	40	Museum	3
Athos	22	Orion and Dryades	4
Attalos	15	Phaedra	32
Ava Apartments & Suites	33	Phidias	23
Byron	34	Philippos	38
Cecil	14	Plaka	20
Central	25	St George Lycabettus	13
Delphi Art Hotel	9	Stratos Vassilikos	18
Electra Palace	27	Student & Traveller's Inn	31
Eridanus	12	Tempi	16
Evropi	8	Thission	24
Exarchion	6	Zinon	10
Feron	2		

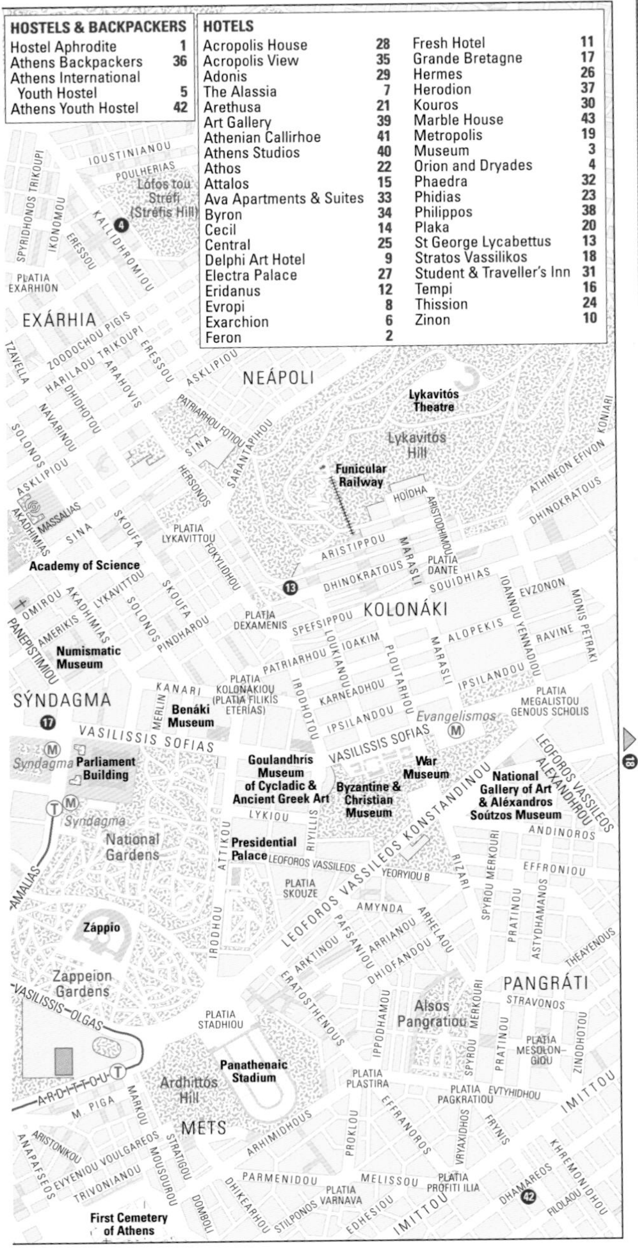

Lófos tou Stréfi (Stréfis Hill)
PLATIA EXARHION
EXÁRHIA
NEÁPOLI
Lykavitós Theatre
Lykavitós Hill
Funicular Railway
PLATIA LYKAVITTOU
Academy of Science
PLATIA DANTE
KOLONÁKI
PLATIA DEXAMENIS
Numismatic Museum
PLATIA KOLONAKIOU (PLATIA FILIKIS ETERIAS)
SÝNDAGMA
Benáki Museum
Evangelismos
PLATIA MEGALISTOU GENOUS SCHOLIS
Syndagma
Parliament Building
Goulandhrís Museum of Cycladic & Ancient Greek Art
Byzantine & Christian Museum
War Museum
National Gallery of Art & Aléxandros Soútzos Museum
National Gardens
Presidential Palace
PLATIA SKOUZE
Záppio
Zappeion Gardens
PANGRÁTI
PLATIA STADHIOU
Alsos Pangratiou
PLATIA MESOLONGIOU
Panathenaic Stadium
Ardhittós Hill
PLATIA PLASTIRA
PLATIA PAGKRATIOU
METS
PLATIA VARNAVA
PLATIA PROFITI ILIA
First Cemetery of Athens
VASILISSIS SOFIAS
LEOFOROS VASSILEOS KONSTANDINOU
LEOFOROS VASSILEOS ALEXANDROU
VASILISSIS OLGAS
ARDITTOU
AMALIAS
IMITTOU

for it – rooms are comfortable with a/c and TV. The rooftop café has a stunning view of the Acropolis and central Athens; breakfast included. €75.

Athos Patröou 3 ☎210 32 21 977, ⓦathoshotel.gr. Metro Sýndagma. Small hotel pleasantly refurbished in 2004, with comfortable, carpeted en-suite rooms (some a little cramped) with TV, a/c, minibar, Internet and all the usual facilities. Also a rooftop bar with Acropolis views. Breakfast included. €80.

Ava Apartments & Suites Lysikrátous 9–11 ☎210 32 59 000, ⓦwww.avahotel .gr. Metro Akrópoli. Between the Temple of Zeus and the Acropolis, *Ava* offers luxurious two-room suites and apartments accommodating up to five people and is ideal for families. All have balconies – some very large – with sideways Acropolis views, as well as small kitchens. €175.

Byron Výronos 19 ☎210 32 30 327, ⓕ210 32 20 276. Metro Akrópoli. Excellent location within walking distance of the Acropolis and Pláka museums, the *Byron* has a/c and TV in every room, plus a few upper rooms with balconies and impressive Acropolis views. Not great value though. €80.

Central Apóllonos 21 ☎210 32 34 357, ⓦwww.centralhotel.gr. Metro Sýndagma. Completely refurbished in designer style, with seagrass or wooden floors, marble bathrooms and excellent soundproofing. Family and interconnecting rooms also available; all with a/c, TV, fridge, Internet connection and everything you'd expect. Large roof terrace with Acropolis views and hot tub. Buffet breakfast included. €120.

Electra Palace Nikodhímou 18 ☎210 33 70 000, ⓦwww.electrahotels.gr. Metro Sýndagma. Luxury hotel right in the heart of Pláka with every facility including both indoor and rooftop pools, small gym and sauna. Stunning if you have an upper-floor suite, whose large balconies have great Acropolis views, but standard rooms are rather dull. €220.

Hermes Apóllonos 19 ☎210 32 35 514, ⓦwww.hermeshotel.gr. Metro Sýndagma. Very classily renovated for the Olympics, with marble bathrooms, polished wood floors and designer touches in every room (plus TV, a/c, fridge and hairdryer)

– some rooms are rather small; others have big balconies. Interconnecting rooms also available. Buffet breakfast included. €120.

Kouros Kódhrou 11 ☎210 32 27 431. Metro Sýndagma. A slightly faded atmospheric *pension*, but with adequate facilities: shared baths and sinks in rooms. Good-value singles. Some balconies overlook the pedestrianized street. €45.

Phaedra Herefóndos 16, cnr Adhrianoú ☎210 32 38 461, ⓕ210 32 27 795. Metro Akrópoli. Simple, newly renovated and quiet at night, thanks to its location at the junction of two pedestrian alleys. Polite, welcoming management; simple rooms with bare tile floors, TV and a/c, not all en-suite (but you get a private bathroom). One of the best deals in Pláka. €55.

Student & Traveller's Inn Kydhathinéon 16 ☎210 32 44 808, ⓦwww .studenttravellersinn.com. Metro Akrópoli. Very friendly, perennially popular travellers' meeting place; a mixture of hotel and hostel. Dorm prices vary, depending on room size and facilities; private quads, triples and doubles, en-suite or shared bath, are clean and comfortable, though not always the quietest. Small courtyard breakfast area/bar, Internet facilities, luggage storage and travel agency. Dorms €16–26, rooms €60.

Monastiráki and Psyrrí

Attalos Athinás 29 ☎210 32 12 801, ⓦwww.attalos.gr. Metro Monastiráki. Modern from the outside but traditional within, the *Attalos* has bright, comfortable rooms, well insulated from the noisy street, all with a/c and TV. Some balcony rooms on the upper floors have great views – there's also a roof-terrace bar in the evenings – but rooms facing the internal courtyard at the back are generally larger and quieter. Some triples. Buffet breakfast available. €80.

Cecil Athinás 39 ☎210 32 17 079, ⓦwww.cecil.gr. Metro Monastiráki. Loving restoration of a run-down 150-year-old *pension*; attractively decorated, good-sized rooms have polished wooden floors, a/c and TV. Helpful management; roof garden; breakfast included. €95.

Metropolis Mitropóleos 46 ☎ 210 32 17 469, ⓦ www.hotelmetropolis.gr. Metro Sýndagma/Monastiráki. Right by the cathedral, the friendly *Metropolis* has simple, plainly furnished rooms with vinyl floors, each with a good-size balcony, a/c and TV, plus Acropolis views from the upper floors; some have shared bathrooms. €55.

Plaka Kapnikaréas 7, cnr Mitropóleos ☎ 210 32 22 096, ⓦ www.plakahotel .gr. Metro Sýndagma/Monastiráki. Excellent location, friendly management and comfortable, quiet refurbished rooms with TV, a/c, and fridge make this a good choice, though popularity means it's often full. The roof garden has particularly good Acropolis views. €130.

Thissío, Gázi and Áno Petrálona

Eridanus Pireós 78 ☎ 210 52 05 360, ⓦ www.eridanus.gr. Metro Thissío. New boutique hotel with every facility including green-marble bathrooms with massage showers. Great Acropolis views from roof terrace and some rooms. Mainly business-oriented, but very good deals sometimes available. €180.

Phidias Apostólou Pávlou 39 ☎ 210 34 59 511, ⓦ www.phidias.gr. Metro Thissío. With an enviable position just down from the *Thission*, the *Phidias* shares similar views, though here only the front rooms have balconies. A little smarter than the *Thission*, with a/c and TV throughout, but still overdue for a makeover. Breakfast included. €80.

Thission Apostólou Pávlou 25 ☎ 210 34 67 634, ⓦ www.hotel-thission.gr. Metro Thissío. Virtually every room at the *Thission* has a balcony with a view of the Acropolis as good as any in Athens, and it lies at the heart of a newly fashionable area crammed with designer cafés. Which makes it even more amazing that nobody has got round to refurbishing the place; rooms are comfortable enough, with a/c and TV, but distinctly threadbare, and service can be slapdash. Great setting, though, and a pleasant roof-terrace café. €70.

Sýndagma and around

Arethusa Mitropóleos 6–8 and Níkis 12 ☎ 210 32 29 431, ⓦ www.arethusahotel .gr. Metro Sýndagma. This low-key, comfortable high-rise caters to independent travellers and small groups. Friendly staff and well-soundproofed, a/c rooms with TV at decent value considering the excellent location. €120.

Grande Bretagne Vasiléos Yioryíou 1, Platía Sýndagma ☎ 210 33 30 000, ⓦ www.grandebretagne.gr. If someone else is paying, try to get them to put you up at the *Grande Bretagne*, the grandest of all Athens' hotels with the finest location in town. Recently refurbished, it really is magnificent, with every conceivable facility. Treatments in the spa cost more than a night at most hotels – rooms are over €300 even for an off-season special offer. €400.

Platía Omonías and the bazaar

The Alassia Sokrátous 50, Omónia ☎ 210 52 74 000, ⓦ www.thealassia .com.gr. Metro Omónia. Refurbished for the Olympics in minimalist style with lots of dark-wood veneers. Rooms are small but well soundproofed (you're just off Platía Omonías here) and with every comfort including designer bathrooms. €110.

Delphi Art Hotel Ayíou Konstandínou 27 ☎ 210 52 44 004, ⓦ www.delphiarthotel .com. Metro Omónia. Right by the National Theatre and Áyios Konstantínos church, this 1930s mansion has been lavishly restored with Art-Nouveau touches and eclectic, individual furnishings. Facilities include Internet access throughout, and Jacuzzi baths in some rooms. Breakfast included. €150.

Evropi Satovriándhou 7 ☎ 210 52 23 081. Metro Omónia. Extremely basic but great-value old-fashioned hotel with spacious rooms occupied only by bed, bedside table and ceiling fan, along with a concrete enclosure for en-suite shower. Reasonably quiet, despite being only a block from Platía Omonías; inexpensive single rooms available. €35.

Fresh Hotel Sofokléous 26 ☎ 210 52 48 511, ⓦ www.freshhotel.gr. Metro

Omónia. Glossy, high-end "designer" hotel in the heart of the market area. Lavish use of colour, designer furnishings and great lighting and bathrooms, though you do wonder how long it will stay looking fresh. Facilities include wireless Internet access throughout and an elegant rooftop pool, bar and restaurant. €190.

Tempi Eólou 29 ℡210 32 13 175, ⊚www.travelling.gr/tempihotel. Metro **Monastiráki**. A longtime favourite with budget travellers: book exchange, drinks and shared kitchen, plus handy affiliated travel agency. Rooms are simple and tiny and most have shared facilities, but the view of the flower market at Ayía Iríni across the quiet pedestrian walkway is enchanting, and it's within walking distance of most central sights. €50.

Zinon Keramikoú 3 and Zínonos ℡210 52 45 711, ⊚www.hotelsofathens.com. Metro **Omónia**. A *Best Western* hotel just off Platía Omonías, the 3-star *Zinon* doesn't look much, but inside has been well refurbished with wireless Internet and flat-screen TVs throughout, and some reasonably priced suites. Substantial discounts sometimes on offer. €110.

The Archeological Museum, Exárhia and Neápoli

Exarchion Themistokléous 55, Platía Exárhia ℡210 38 01 256, ℻210 38 03 296. Metro **Omónia**. Big 1960s high-rise hotel that's a great deal less fancy inside than you might imagine. Vinyl-floored rooms, all with TV, a/c and fridge, are simply furnished and due for refurbishment. But that's reflected in the price, and it's good value if you want to be at the heart of Exárhia's nightlife. Upper-floor rooms are quieter, with better views. €60.

Feron Férron 43, at Ahárnon, Platía Viktorías ℡210 82 32 083. Metro **Viktorías**. As cheap a hotel as any in Athens, and if you expect what you pay for you won't be disappointed. Large, simple, en-suite rooms with ceiling fans. €35.

Museum Bouboulínas 16 ℡210 38 05 611, ⊚www.hotelsofathens.com. Metro

Viktorías/Omónia. Very pleasant, international-style hotel (part of the *Best Western* chain) right behind the National Archeological Museum and the Polytekhnío. Rooms in the new wing, which has triples, quads and small suites ideal for families, are better but slightly more expensive. €135.

Orion and Dryades Anexartisías 5 ℡210 36 27 362, ⊛orion-dryades@mail.com. Metro **Omónia**. Quiet, well-run twin hotels across from the Lófos Stréfi park – a steep uphill walk from almost anywhere. Reception is in the cheaper *Orion*, which has shared bathrooms, a kitchen, and communal area on the roof with an amazing view of central Athens. All rooms in the *Dryades* are en-suite with a/c and TV. €35–65.

Kolonáki and Lykavitós Hill

St George Lycabettus Kleoménous 75, Kolonáki ℡210 72 90 711, ⊚www .sglycabettus.gr. Metro **Evangelismós**. A luxury boutique hotel and an Athenian classic, with a position high on Lykavitós Hill in ritzy Kolonáki overlooking the city. Abundant marble and leather in the public areas plus a very pleasant rooftop pool, and bars and restaurant popular with wealthy young Athenians. Some of the rooms are rather small, however, and there's no point staying here if you don't pay extra for the view. €145 for courtyard view, €220 looking out on the Acropolis.

Stratos Vassilikos Michalakópoulou 114, Ilísia ℡210 77 06 611, ⊚www.airotel.gr. Metro **Mégaro Mousikís**. Predominantly a business hotel, but very comfortable, newly renovated and with all the facilities you'd expect, including satellite TV and Internet in the rooms, marble bathrooms, and even a tiny gym. Good metro and bus connections from its location near the US embassy. Large discounts often available. €220.

Makriyiánni, Koukáki, Pangráti and Mets

Acropolis View Webster 10, Koukáki ℡210 92 17 303, ⊚www.acropolisview .gr. Metro **Akrópoli**. Small but well-furnished rooms with a/c, TV, fridge and tiny marble bathrooms in what looks like a 1970s apartment block. The roof garden has an amazing close-up view of the Acropolis as do some of the rooms if you lean off the balcony. Breakfast included. €65.

Art Gallery Erekthíou 5, Koukáki ☎210 92 38 376, ⊛www.artgalleryhotel.gr. **Metro Syngroú-Fix.** A family-owned converted apartment block, this popular, slightly old-fashioned *pension* with many repeat customers is named for the original artworks that adorn every room. Knowledgeable and helpful staff, convenient location just a short walk from the metro, and a bountiful breakfast (at extra cost) served on a sunny terrace with Acropolis view. €100.

Athenian Callirhoe Kalliróis 32, cnr Petmeza ☎210 92 15 353, ⊛www .tac.gr. **Metro Syngroú-Fix.** Between Koukáki and the centre, the *Callirhoe* was one of Athens' first "designer" hotels. It's already starting to look slightly faded, but central location and good facilities – including TV and Internet in the rooms and a small gym – make it popular with business and leisure travellers alike. Worth checking for offers. €180.

Athens Studios Veïkóu 3a, Makriyiánni, ☎210 92 24 044, ⊛www.athensstudios .gr. Furnished apartments for up to six people, with kitchen, sitting room, TV, phone, a/c and linen provided. Run by the people who run *Athens Backpackers* (see "Hostels"), and including use of their bar and facilities. Great value for groups. From €100 per apartment.

Herodion Robérto Gálli 4 ☎210 92 36 832, ⊛www.herodion.gr. **Metro Akrópoli.** Lovely hotel – not quite as luxurious as the exterior and lobby might lead you to believe – in an enviable position right behind the Acropolis. Comfortable rooms with all facilities and a roof terrace looking almost straight down to the south slope of the Acropolis. €250.

Marble House Cul-de-sac off A. Zínni 35a, Koukáki ☎210 92 34 058, ⊛www .marblehouse.gr. **Metro Syngroú-Fix.** The best value in Koukáki, family run and friendly. Simple rooms with and without private bath, some of them with a/c (for extra charge); also two self-catering studios for long stays. Often full, so call ahead. €42.

Philippos Mitséon 3, Makriyiánni ☎210 922 36111, ⊛www.philipposhotel.gr. **Metro Akrópoli.** Sister hotel to the *Herodion*, the *Philippos* was also completely renovated for the Olympics though the interior is much less dramatic than the new facade. Very comfortable, well-appointed rooms with TV, a/c, minibar and hairdryer. €190.

Around Athens

Acropole Goúnari 7, Pireás ☎210 41 73 313, ⊛www.acropole-hotel.gr. See map on p.140. Perhaps the pick of the hotels in the Pireás port area, this newly renovated place has a variety of rooms including triples; some with Jacuzzi. Breakfast room (breakfast is extra) and bar downstairs. €60.

Astir Palace Vouliagmeni Apóllonos 40, Vouliagméni ☎210 89 02 000, ⊛www .astir-palace.gr. The *Astir Palace* resort complex occupies some 75 acres of a private, pine-covered peninsula, 25km from downtown. There are three separate hotels (least expensive the *Aphrodite*, best probably the designer-style *Nafsika*), plus private villas, pools, water sports, tennis courts and no fewer than six restaurants, with a spa under construction. A shuttle bus runs twice daily to central Athens, just in case the weather prevents you using the helipad. Can at times be dominated by groups attending conferences hosted here. From €290.

Kefalari Suites Pendélis 1, Kifissiá ☎210 62 33 333, ⊛www.kefalari suites.gr. See map on p.144. A dozen luxurious suites, each with its own decorative theme and with every facility you might want. A very long way from the bustle of central Athens. From €180.

Palmyra Beach Possidhónos 70, Glyfádha ☎210 89 81 183, ⊛www .palmyra.gr. Tram Páleo Dimarhío. Well-run, mid-scale tourist hotel with a small pool. The beach of the name isn't up to much, but the hotel is in walking distance of the centre of Glyfádha – handy for the tram – and has plenty of other beaches nearby. There's a free shuttle from the airport during the day, plus the X96 airport express bus stops nearby. Breakfast included. €100.

Hostels and backpackers

There are only a couple of officially recognized hostels in Athens but a number of places, including several of the cheaper hotels listed above, offer beds in shared rooms. We've specified where this is the case.

Hostel Aphrodite Inárdhou 12, between Alakmenous and Mikhaïl Vódha ☎210 88 39 249, ⓦwww.hostelaphrodite .com. Metro Viktorías. Friendly, clean, IYHA-recognized hostel with some private en-suite double and triple rooms, in a quiet residential neighbourhood. A/c available at extra charge, and other facilities including breakfast room/bar, luggage storage and Internet access. Dorms €14, bed in two-bed dorm €22, rooms €40; discounts for YHA card-holders.

Athens Backpackers Mákri 12, Makriyiánni ☎210 92 24 044, ⓦwww .backpackers.gr. Very central Athenian–Australian-run backpackers with few frills, but clean rooms, communal kitchen, Internet access, bar, fabulous rooftop view and great atmosphere. Dorms €18–22.

Athens International Youth Hostel Víktoros Ougó 16 ☎ & ⓕ210 52 32 540. Metro Metaxouryío. The old official youth hostel (it's still official, but no longer the only one) is a huge affair, with 140 beds over 7 floors in 2- and 4-bed rooms. Frayed at the edges and badly in need of a coat of paint, it is cheap and always busy. To be sure of a bed it's best to book in advance and this is essential if you want a private room – do it online at the hostel association website ⓦwww.hihostels.com. Dorm €8.15, plus €2.50 per day for non-members.

Athens Youth Hostel Dhamáreos 75, Pangráti ☎210 75 19 530, ⓦwww .athens-yhostel.com. Trolleys #2 and #11 from Omónia via Sýndagma; bus #203 or #204 (or 15–20min walk) from Metro Evangelismós. A bit out of the way but friendly, with no curfew and in a decent, quiet neighbourhood with plenty of local restaurants. Free use of kitchen and communal area with TV; charge for washing machine and hot water. There's no sign on the door, so look for the green gate. Basic 5/6 bed dorms €12.

Campsites

The city's **campsites** are out in the suburbs and not especially cheap – they're only really worth using if you have a camper van to park. Phone ahead in season to book space.

Athens Camping Leofóros Athinón 198 ☎210 58 14 114, ⓕ210 58 20 353. The closest campsite to the centre of Athens, right by a big main road, but friendly and about as good as you could hope for.

Facilities include a minimarket, restaurant and plenty of hot water. Bus #B16 from Platía Eleftherías or #A15 or #B15 from Platía Karaïskáki.

Camping Nea Kifissia ☎210 80 75 579. More pleasant than *Athens Camping*, but much further out in the cool, leafy suburb of Adames, with a very welcome swimming pool and plenty of other facilities. Take the metro to Kifissiá and transfer onto bus #522/3 to the stop close to the campsite.

Essentials

Arrival

A new airport and substantial investment in transport links have transformed arriving in Athens. The airport is linked to the city by bus, metro and a fast expressway, while the metro, plenty of taxis and city buses service Pireás for those arriving by boat. Even driving in is relatively straightforward thanks to the new roads – though parking or getting around the centre by car is only for the brave.

By air

Athens' **Elefthéríos Venizélos** airport (❽ www.aia.gr) at Spáta, 33km southeast of the city, opened in 2001. Facilities include **ATMs** and banks with **money-changing** facilities on all levels and **luggage storage** with Pacific (☏ 210 35 30 160) on the Arrivals level. There's also the usual array of travel agencies and car-rental places, plus a very handy official **EOT tourist office** (Mon–Sat 9am–7pm, Sun 10am–4pm; ☏ 210 35 30 445) on the Arrivals level. Finally there's a one-room **museum** displaying artefacts discovered in the area – mainly during construction of the airport – which is much more interesting than you might expect.

Public transportation from the airport is excellent. The metro and suburban trains share a station. The **Metro** (line 3; €6 single, €10 return, discounts for multiple tickets) is usually more convenient, taking you straight into the heart of the city where you can change to the other metro lines at either Monastiráki or Sýndagma: trains run every half-hour from 6.30am to 11.30pm, and take around thirty minutes. The **suburban train** runs to Laríssis station and is not quite so handy for the centre of town; it is, though, more comfortable and runs longer hours (5.50am–1.20am) for identical fares. For most of the day it runs every half-hour, with 20 and 50 minutes past the hour, with a journey time of around forty minutes.

Buses are much slower, especially at rush hours, but they're also much cheaper, run all night and offer direct links to other parts of the city including Pireás. The most useful are the #X95 to Sýndagma square, via Ethnikí Ámyna metro and the *Hilton* (at least three an hour, day and night) and #X96 to the port at Pireás via Glyfádha and the beach suburbs (at least two an hour, day and night); others include the #X93 to the bus stations and #X92 to the northern suburb of Kifissiá. Tickets cost €3.20: you can buy them from a booth beside the stops or on the bus – make sure you have small change. Monthly passes are also valid.

Taxis are subject to the vagaries of traffic and can take anything from forty minutes (at night) to an hour and forty minutes (at rush hour) to reach the centre; the fare should be roughly €20–30 to central Athens or Pireás.

By ferry

The simplest way to get to Athens from Pireás is by metro. Trains run from 6am to midnight. For the airport, take express bus #E96 (every 20min 7am–9pm, every 40min 9pm–7am). Taxis between Pireás and central Athens should cost around €8, including baggage: getting a taxi when a ferry arrives is no easy matter, though – you'll need to be pushy, and almost certainly have to share.

City transport

Athens is served by slow but ubiquitous **buses**, a fast, mostly modern **metro** system, and a **tram** service that runs from the centre to the beach suburbs. **Taxis** are also plentiful and, for short journeys in town, exceptionally cheap. Most public transportation operates from around 5am to midnight, with just a few buses – including those to the airport – continuing all night. Driving is a traffic-crazed nightmare, and parking far worse. If you do have a car, you're strongly advised to find somewhere to park it for the duration of your stay and not attempt to use it to get around the city centre.

The metro

The expanded **metro** system is much the easiest way to get around central Athens; it's fast, quiet and user-friendly. It consists of three lines: **Line 1** (green; Pireás to Kifíssiá) is the original section, with useful stops in the centre at Thissío, Monastiráki, Omónia and Viktorías; **Line 2** (red; Áyios Antónios to Áyios Dhimítrios), has central stops at Omónia, Sýndagma and Akrópoli at the foot of the Acropolis; and **Line 3** (blue; Monastiráki to the airport) passes through Sýndagma. Further extensions to lines 2 and 3 are underway, and likely to open in stages over the next few years. Some of the

Tickets and passes

The easiest and least stressful way to travel is with a **pass**. A one-day *imerísio* costs €3 and can be used on buses, trolleybuses, trams and the metro in central Athens. You validate it once, on starting your first journey, and it is good for 24 hours from then. A weekly pass for all the above costs €10; again it must be validated on first use. Monthly passes cost €17.50 for buses only, €35 for bus and metro, or €38 for bus, metro and tram – these are also valid on airport buses. Passes can be bought from any metro ticket office and many places where bus tickets are sold (see below) – you can buy several daily passes at once and then cancel them as necessary.

A ninety-minute €1 ticket is valid on all city-centre transport for ninety minutes from validation. Otherwise, normal **metro tickets** cost €0.70 on Line 1 for journeys of no more than two of its three zones (this will get you from the centre to either end of the line), €0.80 for any other journey (valid for 90min from validation, for travel in one direction – for example you can change lines, but you can't go somewhere and come back). They're available from machines and ticket offices in any metro station, and must be validated before you start your journey, in the machines at the top of the stairs.

Bus tickets cost €0.50 or €0.70 and must be bought in advance from kiosks, certain shops and newsagents, or from the limited number of booths run by bus personnel near major stops – look for the brown, red and white logo proclaiming *Isitíria edhó* ("Tickets here"). They're sold individually or in bundles of ten, and must be validated in the machine on board the bus. €0.50 tickets apply only to a single journey and vehicle; €0.70 include transfers and are valid for ninety minutes from validation.

Tram tickets are sold at machines on the stations. They cost €0.60, or €0.40 if your journey is less than five stops or you're transferring from another form of transport within ninety minutes. Tickets can be validated at machines on the platform or on board.

On any of the above, fare-dodgers risk an on-the-spot **fine** equivalent to forty times the current fare.

new stations are attractions in their own right, displaying artefacts discovered in their excavation (numerous important discoveries were made) and other items of local interest – Sýndagma and Akrópoli are particularly interesting central ones.

Trains run from roughly 5.30am to midnight. When travelling on the metro you need to know the final stop in the direction you're heading, as that is how the platforms are identified ("To Pireás" for example); there are plenty of maps in the stations.

Buses and trolleys

Athens' **bus network** is extensive and cheap, but pretty confusing. Buses are very crowded at peak times, unbearably hot in summer and chronically plagued by strikes and slow-downs; walking is often a better option. Express services run to and from the airport – see p.179. Other routes, where relevant, are detailed in the text. The most straightforward are the **trolleybuses**: #1 connects the Laríssis train station with Omónia, Sýndagma and Koukáki; #2, #4, #5, #9, #11 and #15 all link Sýndagma with Omónia and the National Archeological Museum on 28 Oktovríou (Patissíon). There are also scores of **city buses**, designated by three-digit numbers and serving countless routes out into the straggling suburbs and beyond; at most of the major stops there are helpful information booths.

The tram

The new **tram** network was finished in a hurry for the 2004 Olympics – sometimes you can tell as it sways over lines that don't seem entirely straight. Nonetheless it's a great way to get to the coastal suburbs and the beach. The tram runs from Leofóros Amalías just off Sýndagma to the coast, where it branches. To the right it heads northwest towards Pireás, terminating at SEF (the Stádhio Eirínis ké Fílias or Peace and Friendship Stadium), an interchange with metro line 1 at Néo Fáliro, and within walking distance of Pireás's leisure harbours. Left, the tram lines run southwest along the coast to Glyfádha. There are effectively three lines – #1, from Sýndagma to SEF; #2, from Sýndagma to Glyfádha; and #3, from SEF to Glyfádha. These numbers are displayed on the front of the tram and are worth checking, as the electronic boards at the stations are erratic. The tram doesn't automatically stop at every station, so push the bell if you're on board, or wave it down if you're on the platform.

Taxis

Athenian **taxis** can seem astonishingly cheap – trips around the city centre will rarely run above €3, which means for a group of three or four they cost little more than the metro. Longer trips are also reasonable value: the airport only costing €20–30 and Pireás €7–10 from the centre – the exact amount determined by traffic and amount of luggage. All officially licensed cars are yellow and have a red-on-white numberplate. You can wave them down on the street, pick them up at ranks in most of the major travel termini and central squares, or get your hotel to call for one.

The **meter** starts at €0.85, with a minimum fare of €1.75: legitimate surcharges that will increase the cost include those for baggage; airport, sea-port or station trips; night-time journeys (midnight to 5am); ordering by phone and so on. Every taxi should display the rates and extra charges in English and Greek.

Make sure the meter is switched on when you get in. If it's "not working", find another taxi. Attempts at overcharging tourists are particularly common with small-hours arrivals at the airport and Pireás. One legitimate way that taxi drivers increase their income is to pick up other passengers along the way. There is no fare-sharing: each passenger (or group of passengers) pays the full fare for their journey. So if you're picked up by an already-occupied taxi, memorize the meter reading at once; you'll pay from that point on, plus the €0.85 initial tariff. When hailing an occupied taxi, call out your destination, so the driver can decide whether you suit him or not.

Information

The Greek National Tourist Office (ⓦ www.gnto.gr) has a central information office at Amalías 26, just off Sýndagma (Mon–Fri 9am–6pm, Sat & Sun 11am–4pm; ☎210 33 10 392, ⓦ www.gnto.gr). This is a useful first stop for information, and they have a good free map as well as information sheets on current opening hours, bus and ferry schedules, and so on. If you are arriving by plane, you can save time by calling in at the similarly well-stocked airport branch.

Useful maps to complement those in this guide include the **Rough Guide City Map** of Athens (ⓦ www .roughguides.com) – full-colour, non-tearable, weatherproof and pocket-sized, detailing attractions, places to shop, eat, drink and sleep, as well as the city streets – or for longer stays, the *A-Z*-style street atlases produced by **Emvelia** (ⓦ www .emvelia.gr) and others. These and more should be available from good local

bookshops and some kiosks: the best source is the top floor of the Elefther-oudakis bookshop at Panepistimíou 17, between Sýndagma and Omónia.

Sources of information on **what's on** in English are somewhat limited. There are some listings in a number of free monthly or weekly publications distributed to hotels, but these are partial and not always accurate; better are the weekly **Athens News** (published Friday; ⓦ www .athensnews.gr), with full movie listings and coverage of most major events, or the daily local edition of the *International Herald Tribune*. Much more exhaustive listings including music, clubs, restaurants and bars, but in Greek only, can be found in local weeklies *Athinorama*, *Exo-dos* or *Time Out Athens*. All of the above can be bought at kiosks anywhere in the city: look out too for the free weekly *Athens Voice* (again, Greek only), copies of which can be picked up in galleries, record shops and the like.

Directory

Airlines Aegean, Óthonos 10 ☎210 33 15 515, reservations ☎801 11 20 000; Air France, Vouliagménis 18, Glyfádha ☎210 96 01 100; Alitalia, Vouliagménis 577 ☎210 99 88 900; American Airlines c/o Goldair, Panepistimíou 15 ☎210 33 11 045; British Airways, Themistokléous 1, Glyfádha ☎210 89 06 666; Delta, Óthonos 4 ☎00800 44 12 9506; easyJet, airport only ☎210 35 30 300; Lufthansa, Zirídhi 10, Maroúsi ☎210 61 75 200; Olympic, ticket office at Fillelínon 15 ☎210 92 67 555, main office at Syngroú 96 ☎210 92 69 111, reservations ☎801 11 44 444; Singapore Airlines, Xenofóndos 9 ☎210 37 28 000; Thai, E. Venizélou 32, Glyfádha ☎210 96 92 012.

Airport enquiries For flight arrivals and departures, and all other airport information ☎210 35 30 000.

Banks and exchange Normal banking hours are Mon–Thurs 8am–2.30pm & Fri 8am–2pm and just about all banks can do exchange during those hours; several banks with longer hours can be found around Sýndagma, plus there are numerous currency-exchange places (generally with worse rates) in Pláka and around Sýndagma, and hotels will change money at a worse rate still. Almost every bank in the centre has an ATM.

Car rental The vast majority of downtown car-rental offices are on Leofóros Syngroú, mostly in the first section close to the

Temple of Olympian Zeus. They include Antena at no. 36–38 ☎210 92 24 000, ⊕www.antena.gr; Avance, no. 40–42 ☎210 92 40 107; Europcar, no. 43 ☎210 92 48 810; Hertz, no. 12 ☎210 92 20 102; Holiday Autos, no. 8 ☎210 92 23 088; Sixt, no.23 ☎210 92 20 121; and Thrifty, no. 25 ☎210 92 43 304. Ilios are at Sólonos 138, between Omónia and Exárhia ☎210 38 31 124. The local companies are generally cheaper; if you turn up in person and compare prices, you can often haggle a better rate.

Cinema Athens is a great place to catch a movie. In summer outdoor screens seem to spring up in every neighbourhood of the city – literally dozens of them – for a quintessentially Greek film-going experience. Tickets are around €7–8 for outdoor screenings, €9–12 for first-run fare at a midtown theatre. Films are almost always shown in the original language with Greek subtitles (a good way to increase your vocabulary, though remember that the original language may not be English). Downtown indoor cinemas are concentrated on the three main thoroughfares connecting Omónia and Sýndagma; and in Ambelókipi, around the junctions of Leofóros Alexándhras and Kifissías. Central and reliable outdoor venues include rooftop Cine Pari, Kydhathinéon 22, Pláka (☎210 32 22 071); Thission, Apostólou Pávlou 7 in Thissío (☎210 34 70 980); Psyrri, Sarrí 40–44, Psyrrí (☎210 32 12 476); Zefyros, Tróön 36 in Áno Petrálona (☎210 34 62 677); and Vox Themistokléous 82, Platía Exarhíon (☎210 33 01 020) and Riviera at Valtetsíou 46 (☎210 38 37 716), both in Exárhia.

Dance The one outstanding dance event worth catching is the Dora Stratou Ethnic Dance Company performing in their own theatre at Arakínthou and Voutié on Filopáppou Hill (☎210 32 44 395, ⊕www .grdance.org). Performances (late May to late Sept Tues–Sat 10.15pm, plus Wed & Sun 8.15pm; €13) combine traditional music, fine choreography and gorgeous costumes. To reach the theatre, follow Dhionysíou Areopayítou along the south flank of the Acropolis until you see the signs. Tickets can almost always be picked up at the door.

Disabled travellers Hotels throughout Athens were refurbished in the run-up to the Olympics, and many have accessible rooms and other facilities. However, the infrastructure of the city is tricky for people in wheelchairs or with limited mobility.

Pavements are rarely smooth and frequently blocked, there are many steep streets, and the ground at most archeological sites is extremely uneven. The new metro has excellent lifts from pavement level direct to the platforms, but often a large gap between the platform and the train.

Doctors and hospitals For emergencies, see below. You'll find a list of hospitals, and a few adverts for English-speaking doctors, in the weekly *Athens News*, or the US embassy website at ⊕www.usembassy .gr has hospital addresses and a long list of practitioners (look under Consular Services). Most doctors speak at least some English, and medical care is generally very good, though nursing and after-care tend to rely on the help of family. The largest central hospital is Evangelismós at Ipsilándhou 45, Kolonáki ☎210 72 01 000 (Metro Evangelismós).

Embassies and consulates Australia, Dhimitríou Soútsou 37 ☎210 87 04 000, ⊕www.ausemb.gr (Metro Ambelókipi); Canada, Ioánnou Yennadhíou 4 ☎210 72 73 400, ⊕www.athens.gc.ca (Metro Evangelismós); Ireland, Vassiléos Konstandínou 7 ☎210 72 32 771, in Pangráti near the Panathenaic Stadium; New Zealand (consul-general), Kifissiás 76, Maroúsi ☎210 69 24 136; South Africa, Kifissiás 60, Maroúsi ☎210 610 6645, ⊕www.southafrica.gr; UK, Ploutárhou 1, Kolonáki ☎210 72 72 600, ⊕www .british-embassy.gr (Metro Evangelismós); US, Vasilíssis Sofías 91 ☎210 72 12 951, ⊕www.usembassy.gr (Metro Mégaro Mousikís).

Emergencies Ambulance ☎166; Fire ☎199; Police ☎100; Tourist police ☎171. English-speaking SOS doctors are on ☎1016, and will attend you in your hotel room – at a price.

Ferries Almost any travel agent in Athens can sell you a ferry ticket, but they don't necessarily represent all companies, so shop around to be sure you're not taking a roundabout route. In Pireás, there's far more choice: unless you want a cabin, there's rarely any need to book ahead.

Festivals The great event of the Greek cultural year is the Hellenic Festival, which encompasses a broad spectrum of cultural events: most famously, ancient Greek theatre (performed, in modern Greek, at the Herodes Atticus Theatre on the south slope of the Acropolis), but also modern theatre, traditional and contemporary dance, classical music, jazz, traditional Greek music and even a smattering of rock shows. Other festival venues include the open-air Lykavitós Theatre, and the two ancient theatres at Epidauros. For the latter, you can buy inclusive trips from Athens from the festival box office, either by coach or boat. If you can, it's worth booking in advance (T210 92 82 900, Wwww.hellenicfestival .gr); programmes are available from tourist offices or from the festival box office in the arcade at Panepistimíou 39, downtown (Mon–Fri 8.30am–4pm, Sat 9am–2.30pm). There are also box offices at the Herodes Atticus Theatre (daily 9am–2pm & 6–9pm) and Epidaurus (Mon–Thurs 9am–2pm & 5–8pm, Fri & Sat 9.30am–9.30pm) for events at those venues only.

Football The three major Athens teams – Panathinaïkós, AEK and Olympiakós – dominate Greek football. Panathinaïkós and AEK play at the Olympic stadium in Maroúsi (Metro Iríni). Olympiakós' home is the Karaïskáki stadium in Néo Fáliro (right opposite the metro, or tram to SEF).

Internet There are plenty of Internet cafés throughout central Athens, charging from €1.50–4 per hour. They generally have fast connections and modern machines, but are often smoky. Some of the more central and reliable are: Bits & Bytes, Kapnikaréas 19, off Adhrianoú, Pláka; Café 4U, Ippokrátous 44, Exárhia (24hr); Easy Internet Café, west side of Platía Syndágmatos above Everest (also in Kiffisiá, again above Everest, at Levídhou cnr Kassavéti); Museum Internet Café, 28 Oktovríou 46 by the Archeological Museum; QuickNet, Gladhstónos 4, Omónia (inexpensive and 24hr).

Money Standard currency in Greece is the euro, divided into 100 leptá (cents). You may still see prices quoted in dhrachmas (the old currency) and many till receipts continue to show the value in both, but the old notes and coins are no longer valid. The major credit cards are accepted virtually everywhere, though perhaps with reluctance at the cheaper tavernas and bars.

Opening hours Traditionally shops and offices open from 8.30 or 9am until 1.30 or 2.30pm, when there is a long break for the hottest part of the day. Most places, except banks and government offices, then reopen in the late afternoon, from about 5.30 to 8.30pm; they're closed on Sundays, and often on Saturday, Monday and Wednesday afternoons. However, increasing numbers of places, especially in the city centre and above all the tourist shops in Pláka, now remain open throughout the day. Hours can also vary between

summer and winter (usually Oct–March & April–Sept).

Pharmacies There are a number of large general pharmacies (farmakía) around Omónia, especially on 28 Oktovríou (Patission) and Panepistimíou; many also sell homeopathic remedies. Bakakos, at Ayíou Konstandínou 3 just off Platía Omonias, is the largest general pharmacy in Athens and stocks just about anything. Standard hours are Mon & Wed 8am–2.30pm, Tues, Thurs & Fri 8am–2pm & 5.30–8.30pm. The weekly Athens News has full listings of pharmacies open out-of-hours every day: a list of these is also on display at many pharmacies, or call T107.

Phones Phonecards (tilekárta) for public phones are available from kiosks and small shops, starting at €3. Phonecard booths are ubiquitous, and calling cards for cheap overseas calls are sold at many kiosks, especially around Omónia.

Post offices (tahydhromía) For ordinary letters and parcels up to 2kg, the branch on Sýndagma (cnr Mitropóleos) is open Mon–Fri 7.30am–8pm, Sat 7.30am–2pm, Sun 9am–1pm. There are machines selling stamps and phonecards. To send heavier parcels, use the post office at Mitrópoleos 60, near the Cathedral (Mon–Fri 7.30am–8pm) or at Koumoundhoúrou 29 by the National Theatre, Omónia. There are also major branches near Omónia at Eólou 100 (the central office for poste restante) and on Platía Kótzia. Queues can be enormous, so be sure you're at the right counter – there are often separate ones (with shorter lines) for stamps and parcels.

Public holidays Official holidays are: January 1; January 6; March 25; the first Monday of Lent (variable Feb/March); Easter weekend (variable March/April); May 1; Pentecost or Whit Monday (fifty days after Easter); August 15; October 28; December 25 and 26. Many Athenians take their holidays at Easter and during August, when some shops and restaurants will be closed.

Smoking Greeks smoke heavily, often in crowded public places such as cafés, restaurants and bars. Public transport is nonsmoking, as are many offices, but only a small minority of places to eat or drink will have effective nonsmoking areas.

Time Greek time is always two hours ahead of Britain. For North America, the difference is seven hours for Eastern Standard Time, ten hours for Pacific Standard Time, with an extra hour plus or minus for those few weeks in April when

Fly Less – Stay Longer!

Rough Guides believes in the good that travel does, but we are deeply aware of the impact of fuel emissions on climate change. We recommend taking fewer trips and staying for longer. If you can avoid travelling by air, please use an alternative, especially for journeys of under 1000km/600miles. And always offset your travel at ⊛www.roughguides.com/climatechange.

one place is on daylight saving and the other isn't.

Tours Most travel agencies (see below) offer a variety of tours out of Athens, as well as day- or half-day tours of the city. The latter normally include a bus drive around the highlights and a guided tour of the Acropolis and its museum for around €30. You could also take the Sunshine Express "Happy Train" ride, which sets out from the Platía Paliás Agorás (on Eólou, just off Adhrianoú) and clatters past most of the major sites for an hour or so (€5, children €3). Alternatively the #400 city bus offers a hop-on, hop-off service passing most major

sites – tickets (€5, purchased on the bus) are valid for 24 hours on all public transport. Major stops are at the Archeological Museum, Sýndagma and Omónia.

Travel agencies There are dozens of travel agencies in the streets of Pláka just off Sýndagma, especially on and around Filellínon and Níkis. Almost all offer tours of the city and further afield, as well as ferry and plane tickets. Among them are Dorkas Travel, Níkis 44 ☎210 32 38 726, ⊛www .dorkas.gr; Magic Travel, Níkis 33 ☎210 32 37 471, ⊛www.magic.gr; and Pacific, Níkis 26 ☎210 32 41 007, ⊛www .pacifictravel.gr.

Chronology

c5000 BC ▷ First Neolithic settlements around the rock of the Acropolis.

c1500 BC ▷ Mycenaean palace-fortress established on the Acropolis – traces of its walls can still be seen.

c1200–600 BC ▷ Following the fall of Mycenae, Athens develops as an independent city-state. Draco's draconian law code is published in 621 BC.

594 BC ▷ Amid growing political unrest, Solon appointed as ruler with a mandate to reduce the power of the city's aristocratic clique. His reforms lay the foundations of democracy.

560 BC ▷ The "tyrant" Peisistratos seizes power; under his populist leadership the wealth, power and influence of Athens grow hugely.

510 BC ▷ Kleisthenes introduces the final elements of Athenian democracy, creating a city-state run by its male citizens.

490 BC ▷ Battle of Marathon. The Athenians and their allies defeat a far larger Persian force.

480 BC ▷ Athens sacked and burned to the ground by the Persians. The same year, the Persians are comprehensively defeated at the naval battle of Salamis, off Athens. Victory brings peace and secures Athens' position as Greece's leading city-state.

480–430 BC ▷ The Golden Age. Under the leadership of Pericles, Athens flourishes in every area. The great buildings on the Acropolis and elsewhere – including the Parthenon – are constructed, and in sculpture, pottery, drama and philosophy the city attains unprecedented heights.

431–404 BC ▷ The Peloponnesian War against perennial enemy Sparta ends in defeat and a long period of gradual decline, though in the following century Athens can still boast the likes of Plato and Aristotle.

338 BC ▷ Philip of Macedon takes control of the city.

146 BC ▷ Roman conquest.

52 AD ▷ St Paul preaches to the Athenians from the Areopagus.

380 ▷ Christianity becomes the official religion of the Roman Empire, now ruled from Byzantium (Constantinople). Athens' temples gradually converted to Christian use; early churches built.

1300–1456 ▷ Athens passes through the hands of various European powers: Franks, Catalans, Florentines and Venetians.

1456 ▷ Sultan Mehmet II conquers Constantinople and takes control of Athens. Under Turkish rule for almost 400 years, Athens is a backwater. The Parthenon and other temples are converted to mosques.

1821 ▷ Greek War of Independence begins.

1828 ▷ First Greek National Assembly held, in Náfplio.

1834 ▷ Capital of Greece moved to Athens by Otto, the new King appointed by the Great Powers. Construction of the modern city begins.

1896 ▷ First modern Olympic Games held in Athens.

1923 ▷ Following a disastrous Greek military campaign in Turkey, the Treaty of Lausanne provides for a massive exchange of populations between Greece and Turkey – over 1,000,000 refugees arrive, many settling in Athens and Pireás.

1941–44 ▷ German occupation; many die of famine in winter of 1941–42.

1944–49 ▷ Greek Civil War.

1967–74 ▷ Colonels' junta sees army seize power.

1973 ▷ Massacre of students at the Athens Polytechnic marks the beginning of the end for the colonels.

1981 ▷ Greece elects socialist government and joins EC.

1990s ▷ First serious attempts to tackle pollution problems. Increasing growth and stability rewarded with the award of the 2004 Olympics.

2004 ▷ Despite last-minute preparations and massive cost over-runs, Olympics are a huge success, with a lasting legacy in terms of infrastructure and transformation of the city's reputation.

Language

Basics

You can get by in Athens speaking only English – in the tourist areas certainly there'll always be someone who can speak it fluently. Away from the centre you may struggle occasionally, but even here an English-speaker is rarely far away. However, the effort of mastering a few Greek words is well repaid, and will transform your status from that of dumb *tourístas* to the more honourable one of *xénos/xéni*, a word which can mean foreigner, traveller and guest all rolled into one.

The Rough Guide *Greek Dictionary Phrasebook* is full of more phrases than you'll need. It also fills you in on cultural know-how and is sensibly transliterated.

Pronunciation

On top of the usual difficulties of learning a new language, Greek presents the additional problem of an entirely separate **alphabet**. Despite initial appearances, this is in practice fairly easily mastered and is a skill that will help enormously if you are going to get around independently. In addition, certain combinations of letters have unexpected results. Remember that the correct **stress** (marked with an accent) is crucial. With the right sounds but the wrong stress people will either fail to understand you, or else understand something quite different from what you intended – there are numerous pairs of words with the same spelling and phonemes, distinguished only by their stress.

Set out below is the Greek alphabet, the system of transliteration used in this book, and a brief aid to pronunciation.

Greek	Transliteration	Pronounced
A, α	a	a as in father
B, β	v	v as in vet
Γ, γ	y/g	y as in yes except before consonants or a, o or ou when it's a breathy g, approximately as in gap
Δ, δ	dh	th as in then
E, ε	e	e as in get
Z, ζ	z	z sound
H, η	i	i as in ski
Θ, θ	th	th as in theme
I, ι	i	i as in ski
K, κ	k	k sound
Λ, λ	l	l sound
M, μ	m	m sound
N, ν	n	n sound
Ξ, ξ	x	x sound
O, o	o	o as in toad

Π, π	p	p sound
Ρ, ρ	r	r sound
Σ, σ, ς	s	s sound, except z before m or g; single sigma has the same phonic value as double sigma
Τ, τ	t	t sound
Υ, υ	y	y as in barely
Φ, φ	f	f sound
Χ, χ	h before vowels,	harsh h sound, like ch in loch, kh before consonants
Ψ, ψ	ps	ps as in lips
Ω, ω	o	o as in toad, indistinguishable from o

Combinations and diphthongs

ΑΙ, αι	e	e as in hey
ΑΥ, αυ	av/af	av or af depending on following consonant
ΕΙ, ει	i	long i, exactly like ι or η
ΕΥ, ευ	ev/ef	ev or ef, depending on following consonant
ΟΙ, οι	i	long i, exactly like ι or η
ΟΥ, ου	ou	ou as in tourist
ΓΓ, γγ	ng	ng as in angle; always medial
ΓΚ, γκ	g/ng	g as in goat at the beginning of a word, ng in the middle
ΜΠ, μπ	b/mb	b at the beginning of a word, mb in the middle
ΝΤ, ντ	d/nd	d at the beginning of a word, nd in the middle
ΤΣ, τσ	ts	ts as in hits
ΤΖ, τζ	tz	dg as in judge, j as in jam in some dialects

Words and phrases

Basics

Né	Yes
Málista	Certainly
Óhi	No
Parakaló	Please
Endáxi	OK, agreed
Efharistó (polý)	Thank you (very much)
(Dhén) Katalavéno	I (don't) understand
Parakaló, mípos	Excuse me
Miláte angliká?	Do you speak English?
Signómi	Sorry, excuse me
Símera	Today
Ávrio	Tomorrow
Khthés	Yesterday
Tóra	Now
Argótera	Later
Anikhtó	Open
Klistó	Closed
Méra	Day
Níkhta	Night

Tó proï	In the morning
Tó apóyevma	In the afternoon
Tó vrádhi	In the evening
Edhó	Here
Eki	There
Aftó	This one
Ekíno	That one
Kaló	Good
Kakó	Bad
Megálo	Big
Mikró	Small
Perisótero	More
Ligótero	Less
Lígo	A little
Polý	A lot
Ftinó	Cheap
Akrivó	Expensive
Zestó	Hot
Krýo	Cold
Mazi (mé)	With (together)
Horís	Without
Grígora	Quickly
Sigá	Slowly

Kýrios/Kyria	Mr/Mrs
Dhespinis	Miss
Trógo/píno	To eat/drink
Foúrnos, psomádhiko	Bakery
Farmakío	Pharmacy
Tahydhromío	Post office
Gramatósima	Stamps
Venzinádhiko	Petrol station
Trápeza	Bank
Leftá/khrímata	Money
Toualéta	Toilet
Astynomía	Police
Yiatrós	Doctor
Nosokomío	Hospital

Requests

To ask a question, it's simplest to start with *parakaló*, then name the thing you want in an interrogative tone.

Parakaló, ó foúrnos?	Where is the bakery?
Parakaló, ó dhrómos yiá . . . ?	Can you show me the road to . . . ?
Parakaló, éna dhomátio yiá dhyo átoma	We'd like a room for two
Parakaló, éna kiló portokália?	May I have a kilo of oranges?
Poú?	Where?
Pós?	How?
Póssi, pósses or póssa?	How many?
Póso?	How much?
Póte?	When?
Yiatí?	Why?
Ti óra . . . ?	At what time . . . ?
Tí íne/Pió íne . . . ?	What is/ Which is . . . ?
Póso káni?	How much does it cost?
Tí óra aníyi?	What time does it open?
Tí óra klíni?	What time does it close?

Conversation

By far the most common greeting, on meeting and parting, is *yiá sou/yiá sas* – literally "health to you". Incidentally, the approaching party utters the first greeting, not those seated at sidewalk *kafenío* tables or doorsteps.

Hérete	Hello
Kalí méra	Good morning
Kalí spéra	Good evening
Kalí níkhta	Good night
Adío	Goodbye
Tí kánis/Tí kánete?	How are you?
Kalá íme	I m fine
Ké essís?	And you?
Pós se léne?	What's your name?
Mé léne . . .	My name is . . .
Parakaló, miláte pió sigá	Speak slower, please
Pós léyete stá Ellínika?	How do you say it in Greek?
Dhén xéro	I don t know
Thá sé dhó ávrio	See you tomorrow
Kalí andhámosi	See you soon
Páme	Let s go
Parakaló, ná mé voithíste	Please help me

Greek's Greek

There are numerous words and phrases which you will hear constantly, even if you rarely have the chance to use them. These are a few of the most common.

Éla!	Come (literally) but also "Speak to me!", "You don't say!", and so on.
Oriste!	Literally, "Indicate!"; in effect, "What can I do for you?"
Embrós! or Léyete!	Standard phone responses.
Tí néa?	What's new?
Tí yínete?	What's going on (here)?
É tsi k'étsi	So-so.
Ó pa!	Whoops! Watch it!
Po-po-po!	Expression of dismay or concern, like French "O là là!".
Pedhí moú	My boy/girl, sonny, friend etc.
Maláka(s)	Literally "wanker", but often used (don't try it!) as an informal term of address.
Sigá sigá	Take your time, slow down.
Kaló taxídhi	Bon voyage.

Accommodation

Xenodhohío	Hotel
Xenón(as)	Inn
Xenónas neótitos	Youth hostel
Éna dhomátio . . .	A room . . . for one/
yiá éna/dhýo/tría	two/ three
átoma...yiá mía/	people...for one/
dhýo/trís vradhiés	two/three nights...
...mé megálo	with a double
kreváti...mé doús	bed... with a
	shower
Zestó neró	Hot water
Krýo neró	Cold water
Klimatismós	Air conditioning
Anamistíra	Fan
Boró ná tó dhó?	Can I see it?
Boroúme na	Can we camp here?
váloume ti skiní	
edhó?	
Kámping/	
Kataskínosi	Campsite
Skiní	Tent

Travel

Aeropláno	Aeroplane
Leoforío, púlman	Bus, coach
Aftokínito, amáxi	Car
Mihanáki, papáki	Motorbike, scooter
Taxí	Taxi
Plío/vapóri/karávi	Ship
Tahýplio	High-speed
	catamaran
Dhelfíni	Hydrofoil
Tréno	Train
Sidhirodhromikós	Train station
stathmós	
Podhílato	Bicycle
Otostóp	Hitching
Mé tá pódhia	On foot
Monopáti	Trail
Praktorío leoforíon,	Bus station
KTEL	
Stássi	Bus stop
Limáni	Harbour
Ti óra févyi?	What time does it
	leave?
Ti óra ftháni?	What time does it
	arrive?
Póssa hiliómetra?	How many
	kilometres?
Pósses óres?	How many hours?
Poú pás?	Where are you
	going?
Páo stó . . .	I'm going to . . .

Thélo ná katévo	I want to get
stó . . .	off at . . .
O dhrómos yiá . . .	The road to . . .
Kondá	Near
Makriá	Far
Aristerá	Left
Dhexiá	Right
Katefthía, ísia	Straight ahead
Éna isitírio yiá . . .	A ticket to . . .
Éna isitírio mé	A return ticket
epistrof	
Paralía	Beach
Spiliá	Cave
Kéndro	Centre (of town)
Eklissía	Church
Thálassa	Sea
Horió	Village

Numbers

énas/éna/mía	1
dhýo	2
trís/tría	3
tésseres/téssera	4
pénde	5
éxi	6
eftá	7
okhtó	8
ennéa (or more slangy,	
enyá)	9
dhéka	10
éndheka	11
dhódheka	12
dhekatrís	13
dhekatésseres	14
íkossi	20
íkossi éna (all compounds	
written separately thus)	21
triánda	30
saránda	40
penínda	50
exínda	60
evdhomínda	70
ogdhónda	80
enenínda	90
ekató	100
ekatón penínda	150
dhiakóssies/dhiakóssia	200
pendakóssies/	
pendakóssia	500
hílies/hília	1000
dhýo hiliádhes	2000
éna ekatomírio	1,000,000
próto	first
dhéftero	second
tríto	third

Days of the week and the time

Kyriakí	Sunday
Dheftéra	Monday
Tríti	Tuesday
Tetárti	Wednesday
Pémpti	Thursday
Paraskeví	Friday
Sávato	Saturday
Ti óra íne?	What time is it?
Mía iy óra/dhýo iy óra/tris iy óra	One/two/ three o'clock
Tésseres pará íkossi	Twenty minutes to four
Eftá ké pénde	Five minutes past seven
Éndheka ké misí	Half past eleven
Sé misí óra	In half an hour
S'éna tétarto	In a quarter-hour
Sé dhýo óres	In two hours

Months and seasons

Note that you may see hybrid forms of the months written on schedules or street signs; the below are the spoken demotic forms.

Yennáris	January
Fleváris	February
Mártis	March
Aprílis	April
Maḯos	May
Ioúnios	June
Ioúlios	July
Ávgoustos	August
Septémvris	September
Októvrios	October
Noémvris	November
Dhekémvris	December
Therinó dhromolóyio	Summer schedule
Himerinó dhromolóyio	Winter schedule

Menu reader

Basics

Aláti	Salt
Avgá	Eggs
(Horís) ládhi	(Without) Oil
Hortofágos	Vegetarian
Katálogo, lísta	Menu
Kréas	Meat
Lahaniká	Vegetables
O logariasmós	The bill
Méli	Honey
Neró	Water
Psári(a)	Fish
Psomí	Bread
Olikís	Wholemeal bread
Sikalísio	Rye bread
Thalassiná	Seafood
Tyrí	Cheese
Yiaoúrti	Yogurt
Záhari	Sugar

Cooking terms

Akhnistó	Steamed
Makaronádha	Any pasta-based dish
Pastó	Marinated in salt
Psitó	Roasted
Saganáki	Cheese-based red sauce; or any fried cheese
Skáras	Grilled
Sti soúvla	Spit-roasted
Stó foúrno	Baked
Tiganitó	Pan-fried
Tís óras	Grilled/fried to order
Yakhní	Stewed in oil and tomato sauce
Yemistá	Stuffed (squid, vegetables, and so on)

Soups and starters

Avgolémono	Egg and lemon soup
Dolmádhes	Stuffed vine-leaves
Fasoládha	Bean soup
Fáva	Purée of yellow peas, served with onion and lemon
Florínes	Canned, red, sweet Macedonian peppers
Hortópita	Turnover or pie stuffed with wild greens
Kafterí	Cheese dip with chili added
Kápari	Pickled caper-leaves
Kopanistí, khtypití	Pungent, fermented cheese purée
Kritamo	Rock samphire
Mavromátika	Black-eyed peas
Melitzanosaláta	Aubergine/eggplant dip
Revytho-keftédhes	Chickpea (garbanzo) patties
Skordhaliá	Garlic dip
Soúpa	Soup
Taramosaláta	Cod-roe paté
Trahanádhes	Crushed wheat and milk soup, sweet or savoury
Tyrokafterí	Cheese dip with chilli, different from *kopanistí*
Tzatzíki	Yoghurt and cucumber dip
Tzirosaláta	Cured mackerel dip

Vegetables

Angináres	Artichokes
Angoúri	Cucumber
Ánitho	Dill
Bámies	Okra, ladies' fingers
Bouréki, bourekákia	Courgette/zucchini, potato and cheese pie
Briám	Ratatouille
Domátes	Tomatoes
Fakés	Lentils
Fasolákia	French (green) beans
Horiátiki (saláta)	Greek salad (with olives, feta etc)
Hórta	Greens (usually wild), steamed
Kolokythákia	Courgette/zucchini
Koukiá	Broad beans
Maroúli	Lettuce
Melitzánes imám	Aubergine/eggplant slices baked with onion, garlic and copious olive oil
Patátes	Potatoes
Piperiés	Peppers
Pligoúri, pinigoúri	Bulgur wheat
Radhíkia	Wild chicory – a common *hórta*
Rýzi, piláfi	Rice (usually with *sáltsa* – sauce)
Rókka	Rocket
Saláta	Salad
Spanáki	Spinach
Vlíta	Notchweed – another common *hórta*
Yígandes	White haricot beans

Fish and seafood

Astakós	Aegean lobster
Atherína	Sand smelt
Bakaliáros	Cod or hake, usually the latter
Barbóuni	Red mullet
Fangrí	Common bream
Foúskes	*Uovo de mare* (Italian), *violet* (French); no English equivalent for this invertebrate.
Galéos	Dogfish, hound shark, tope
Garídhes	Shrimp, prawns
Gávros	Mild anchovy
Glóssa	Sole
Gónos, gonákia	Any hatchling fish
Gópa	Bogue
Kalamarákia	Baby squid
Kalamária	Squid
Karavídhes	Crayfish
Kefalás	Axillary bream
Koliós	Chub mackerel
Koutsomoúra	Goatfish (small red mullet)
Kydhónia	Cockles
Lakérdha	Light-fleshed bonito, marinated
Marídhes	Picarel
Melanoúri	Saddled bream
Ménoula	Sprat
Mýdhia	Mussels
Okhtapódhi	Octopus
Pandelís	Corvina; also called *sykiós*

Platý	Skate, ray
Sardhélles	Sardines
Sargós	White bream
Seláhi	Skate, ray
Skáros	Parrotfish
Skathári	Black bream
Skoumbrí	Atlantic mackerel
Soupiá	Cuttlefish
Spiníalo, spinóalo	Marinated *foúskes*
Synagrídha	Dentex
Tsipoúra	Gilt-head bream
Vátos	Skate, ray
Xifías	Swordfish
Yermanós	Leatherback

Meat dishes

Arní	Lamb
Bekrí mezé	Pork chunks in red sauce
Biftéki	Hamburger
Brizóla	Pork or beef chop
Hirinó	Pork
Keftédhes	Meatballs
Kokorétsi	Liver/offal roulade, spit-roasted
Kopsídha	Lamb shoulder chops
Kotópoulo	Chicken
Kounélli	Rabbit
Loukánika	Spicy course-ground sausages
Moskhári	Veal
Moussakás	Aubergine, potato and lamb-mince casserole with béchamel topping
Païdhákia	Rib chops, lamb or goat
Papoutsákia	Stuffed aubergine/ eggplant "shoes" – like *moussakás* without béchamel
Pastítsio	Macaroni pie baked with minced meat
Pastourmás	Cured, highly spiced meat; traditionally camel, nowadays beef
Patsás	Tripe and trotter soup
Psaronéfri	Pork tenderloin medallions
Salingária	Garden snails
Soutzoukákia	Minced-meat rissoles/beef patties
Spetzofáï	Sausage and pepper stew

Stifádho	Meat stew with tomato and onions
Sykóti	Liver
Tiganiá	Meat chunks, usually pork, fried in its own fat
Tziyéro sarmás	Lamb's liver in cabbage
Youvétsi	Baked-clay casserole of meat and *kritharáki* (short pasta)

Sweets and desserts

Baklavá	Honey and nut pastry
Bougátsa	Salt- or sweet- cream pie served warm with sugar and cinnamon
Galaktobóureko	Custard pie
Halvás	Sweetmeat of sesame or semolina
Karydhópita	Walnut cake
Kréma	Custard
Loukoumádhes	Dough fritters in honey syrup and sesame seeds
Pagotó	Ice cream
Pastélli	Sesame and honey bar
Ravaní	Spongecake, lightly syruped
Ryzógalo	Rice pudding

Fruit and nuts

Akhládhia	Big pears
Aktinídha	Kiwis
Fistíkia	Pistachio nuts
Fráoules	Strawberries
Karpoúzi	Watermelon
Kerásia	Cherries
Krystália	Miniature pears
Kydhóni	Quince
Lemónia	Lemons
Míla	Apples
Pepóni	Melon
Portokália	Oranges
Rodhákino	Peach
Sýka	Figs
Stafýlia	Grapes

Cheese

Ayeladhinó	Cow's-milk cheese
Féta	Salty, white cheese

Graviéra	Gruyère-type hard cheese
Katsikisio	Goat cheese
Kasséri	Medium-sharp cheese
Myzíthra	Sweet cream cheese
Próvio	Sheep's cheese

Drinks

Alisfakiá	Island sage tea
Boukáli	Bottle
Býra	Beer
Gála	Milk
Frappé	Iced coffee
Galakakáo	Chocolate milk

Gazóza	Generic fizzy drink
Kafés	Coffee
Krasí	Wine
áspro	white
kokkinélli/rozé	rosé
kókkino/mávro	red
Limonádha	Lemonade
Metalikó neró	Mineral water
Portokaládha	Orangeade
Potíri	Glass
Stinyássas!	Cheers!
Tsáï	Tea
Tsáï vounoú	"Mountain" (mainland sage) tea

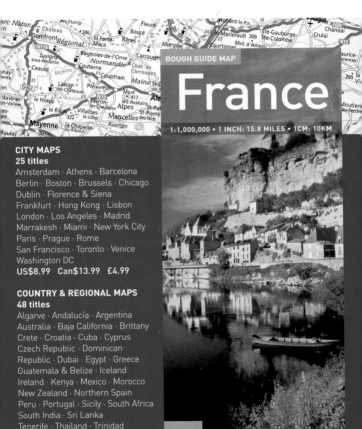

Rough Guides To A World Of Music

'stick to the reliable Rough Guide series' **The Guardian (UK)**

Greece is located at one of the most important cultural crossroads in the world, so it is only natural that both East and West have influenced contemporary Greek music. The amazingly varied repertoire of this country is presented on this Rough Guide from the traditional to the contemporary, from the distinctly eastern, blues-like *rembetika*, to the orchestrated folk sounds of *entechno* music through to the tough, gritty sounds of the popular *laiko*.

THE ROUGH GUIDE TO THE MUSIC OF GREECE

THE ROUGH GUIDE TO REBÉTIKA

Greece

Rebétika

MUSIC ROUGH GUIDE
ENHANCED CD

rembetika and folk songs of the near east

MUSIC ROUGH GUIDE

the Greek underworld: original roots to revival sounds

Rebétika is the music of the Greek underworld, whose golden years started shortly after Greek national independence and lasted until the 1950s. A rich and heady stew, *rebétika* focuses on hopeless love, disease, drugs, death and imprisonment. As a musical form, it draws on numerous sources such as the formal instrumental suites of the Ottoman court, the solo vocals of Turkey and Iran, and the captivating, sophisticated instrumentation of the *café aman* in Istanbul and Izmir. *The Rough Guide To Rebétika* showcases some of the best *rebétika* artists from its early roots to the rising stars of the more recent revival movement.

Hear sound samples at WWW.VVoRLDMusic.NeT

Rough Guides Radio

Now you can visit www.worldmusic.net/radio to tune into the exciting Rough Guide Radio Show, with a new show each month presenting new releases, interviews, features and competitions.

Available from book and record shops worldwide or order direct from World Music Network, 6 Abbeville Mews, 88 Clapham Park Road, London SW4 7BX, UK
T. 020 7498 5252   F. 020 7498 5353   E. post@worldmusic.net

small print & **Index**

SMALL PRINT

A Rough Guide to Rough Guides

In 1981, Mark Ellingham, a recent graduate in English from Bristol University, was travelling in Greece on a tiny budget and couldn't find the right guidebook. With a group of friends he wrote his own guide, combining a contemporary, journalistic style with a practical approach to travellers' needs. That first Rough Guide was a student scheme that became a publishing phenomenon. Today, Rough Guides include recommendations from shoestring to luxury and cover hundreds of destinations around the globe, including almost every country in the Americas and Europe, more than half of Africa and most of Asia and Australasia. Millions of readers relish Rough Guides' wit and inquisitiveness as much as their enthusiastic, critical approach and value-for-money ethos. The guides' ever-growing team of authors and photographers is spread all over the world.

In the early 1990s, Rough Guides branched out of travel, with the publication of Rough Guides to World Music, Classical Music and the Internet. All three have become benchmark titles in their fields, spearheading the publication of a range of more than 350 titles under the Rough Guide name, including phrasebooks, waterproof maps, music guides from Opera to Heavy Metal, reference works as diverse as Conspiracy Theories and Shakespeare, and popular culture books from iPods to Poker. Rough Guides also produce a series of more than 120 World Music CDs in partnership with World Music Network.

Visit www.roughguides.com to see our latest publications.

Rough Guide travel images are available for commercial licensing at www.roughguidespictures.com

Publishing information

This second edition published March 2007 by Rough Guides Ltd, 80 Strand, London WC2R 0RL. 345 Hudson St, 4th Floor, New York, NY 10014, USA.

Distributed by the Penguin Group
Penguin Books Ltd, 80 Strand, London WC2R 0RL
Penguin Group (USA), 375 Hudson St, NY 10014, USA
14 Local Shopping Centre, Panchsheel Park, New Delhi 110017, India
Penguin Group (Australia), 250 Camberwell Rd, Camberwell, Victoria 3124, Australia
Penguin Group (Canada), 10 Alcorn Av, Toronto, ON M4V 1E4, Canada
Penguin Group (NZ), 67 Apollo Drive, Mairangi Bay, Auckland 1310, New Zealand

Typeset in Bembo and Helvetica to an original design by Henry Iles.

Cover concept by Peter Dyer.

Printed and bound in China
© John Fisher 2007

212pp includes index

A catalogue record for this book is available from the British Library

ISBN 10: 1-84353-773-7

ISBN 13: 9-781-84353-773-1

The publishers and authors have done their best to ensure the accuracy and currency of all the information in Athens DIRECTIONS, however, they can accept no responsibility for any loss, injury, or inconvenience sustained by any traveller as a result of information or advice contained in the guide.

1   3   5   7   9   8   6   4   2

Help us update

We've gone to a lot of effort to ensure that the second edition of Athens DIRECTIONS is accurate and up-to-date. However, things change – places get "discovered", opening hours are notoriously fickle, restaurants and rooms raise prices or lower standards. If you feel we've got it wrong or left something out, we'd like to know, and if you can remember the address, the price, the phone number, so much the better.

We'll credit all contributions, and send a copy of the next edition (or any other DIRECTIONS guide or Rough Guide if you prefer) for the best letters. Everyone who writes to us and isn't already a subscriber will receive a copy of our full-colour thrice-yearly newsletter. Please mark letters: "Athens DIRECTIONS Update" and send to: Rough Guides, 80 Strand, London WC2R 0RL, or Rough Guides, 4th Floor, 345 Hudson St, New York, NY 10014. Or send an email to mail@roughguides.com

Have your questions answered and tell others about your trip at www.roughguides.atinfopop.com

Rough Guide credits

Text editor: Lucy White
Layout: Jessica Subramanian
Cartography: Katie Lloyd-Jones
Picture editor: Mark Thomas

Production: Aimee Hampson
Proofreader: Diane Margolis
Cover design: Diana Jarvis
Photographer: Michelle Grant

SMALL PRINT

The author

John Fisher co-authored the first edition of the *Rough Guide to Greece* – the first Rough Guide ever – and has been inextricably linked with Rough Guides ever since. He lives in South London with his wife and two sons.

Acknowledgements

As ever, thanks are due to far more people than can be listed here, but above all to Kate Donnelly, Nick Edwards and his Athens crew, Miranda Rashidian, Panos Zisimatos, everyone at Rough Guides, and all of you who wrote in with updates and suggestions – keep 'em coming. Above all, as ever to A and the two Js for love and support.

Photo credits

All images © Rough Guides except the following:

p.18 Icon of the Virgin © Robert Harding/Alamy
p.20 Statue of Poseidon © Vanni Archive/Corbis
p.20 Fresco in the National Archaeological Museum © Peter Norree/Alamy
p.21 Gold Vafio Cup © Gianni Dagli Orti/Corbis
p.21 The Little Jockey © John Kolesidis/Corbis
p.29 Spring flowers © John Fisher
p.35 Herodes Atticus Theatre © IML Image Group/Alamy
p.35 Lykavitós Theatre © Dorling Kindersley

p.41 Easter ceremony © David Sanger photography/Alamy
p.44 Temple of Afaia © John Fisher
p.131 The Old Olympic Stadium, Athens © Corbis
p.134 The residential area of Pangráti © Pixida/Alamy
p.150 Shopping in Kifissiá © Doifel/Alamy
p.158 Temple of Zeus, Delphi © Jon Arnold Images/Alamy
p.159 Corinth © Rolf Richardson/Alamy

Index

Maps are marked in colour

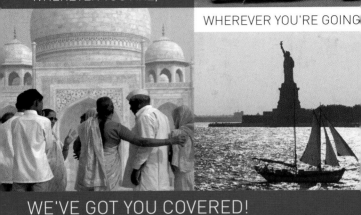